Georg Büchner
COMPLETE PLAYS AND PROSE

Georg Büchner

COMPLETE PLAYS AND PROSE

Translated and with an Introduction by
CARL RICHARD MUELLER

A MERMAID DRAMABOOK
HILL AND WANG · NEW YORK

Manufactured in the United States of America
by The Colonial Press Inc., Clinton, Massachusetts

12   13   14   15   16

For
Jay, Lynn, and John-Paul Varela,
whose friendship is
more precious
than this volume can ever
even partially
repay

ACKNOWLEDGMENTS

It is with considerable gratitude that I acknowledge my debt to the Fulbright Commission for awarding me a Study Grant for the year 1960–1961, the greater part of which was spent in Berlin, and during which most of this volume in its early stages was prepared. My thanks, too, to Arthur W. Wang, without whose bold concern for great drama of all ages this first wholly complete edition of the works of Georg Büchner in the English language would not have been possible.

C.R.M.

CONTENTS

CONTENTS

INTRODUCTION

Beginnings

Suffice it to say of the life of Georg Büchner that it was short, intense, and tragic. Born on October 17, 1813, in the small German town of Goddelau, Georg soon came under the very individual influence of his father, physician in government service who was a confirmed rationalist and an admirer of Napoleon. Georg, he had decided, would become a physician, like himself. The boy did indeed possess a naturally inquiring mind of a strongly scientific bent, a mind which sought out reality in all things, including literature. He at first embarked on a course of medical studies at Strasbourg, in 1831, but in 1833 shifted to Giessen, where he concentrated on philosophy and history. Here he composed the revolutionary tract *The Hessian Courier*, and became so deeply involved in political struggle that he had to flee the country. After making his way to Zurich, he decided that at that particular time all revolutionary activity was in vain.

During the next, and final, few years of his life, this young scientist, preparing himself for research and teaching at the University of Zurich and never dreaming of playwriting as a career, wrote three plays, two of them so extraordinary that they have served as the impetus for literary movements down to the present day's Theatre of the Absurd. Theodore Hoffman has recently listed them as: Naturalism, Social Realism, Psychological Irrationalism, Expressionism, and Existential Theatre. He is the seemingly inexhaustible source of modern drama and has been universally extolled by the leaders of the aforementioned movements. And yet, though he was far ahead of his own time, and though he sank into virtual oblivion after his death, until his rediscovery by the first of the great Naturalist playwrights, Gerhart Hauptmann, he is still in advance of our own age. Only time will demonstrate what new movements he will father for future generations.

His life was short, his life was tragic. He always said it would be. He died at the age of twenty-three years and four months, on February 19, 1837, of an undiagnosed fever, which may have been typhus.

Danton's Death

In *Danton's Death* we have undoubtedly the finest first play ever written. It is powerful, relentless, inexorable, passionate, and personal—it is as bitter a philosophical statement as anyone since Sophocles has had the courage to put on a stage—and finally, despite much critical assertion that it lacks drama, it is dramatic in spite of itself.

Danton's Death is pervaded by one single concept, the leading obsession in all of Büchner's works, in his daily life and his correspondence; he is never tired of reiterating that there is no free will, that Man's destiny is determined. In *Danton* he takes the direct and easy way of declaring this doctrine: by preaching—but, after all, it was his first play; in *Leonce and Lena* it has been hidden beneath the deceptive surface of quite literary, derivative, but in the final analysis highly original, parody; and in *Woyzeck* it is ingeniously unstated, but always present in its implicit dramatic manifestation.

Man is not free—History is a relentless force which crushes Man—all action is futile—boredom with the sameness of existence is the universal curse. For so young a man as Büchner (he was twenty-one when he wrote *Danton*) these are somewhat explosive ideas to be toying with. And yet he came by them some years earlier as a result of research into the history of the French Revolution of 1789. According to Büchner's major German critic-editor Fritz Bergemann, the following letter to his fiancée was written possibly late in 1833, two years prior to the actual composition of *Danton's Death*, a task accomplished, as Büchner tells us, in a period of less than five weeks, for the sake of making money. These are his words:

For several days now I have taken every opportunity of taking pen in hand, but have found it impossible to put down so much as a single word. I have been studying the history of the Revolution. I have felt as though crushed beneath the fatalism of History. I find in human nature a terrifying sameness, and in the human condition an inexorable force, granted to all and to none. The individual is no more than foam on the wave, greatness mere chance, the mastery of genius a puppet play, a ludicrous struggle against a brazen law, which to acknowledge is the highest achievement, which to master, impossible. I no longer intend to bow down to the parade horses and the bystanders of History. I have grown accustomed to the sight of blood. But I am no guillotine blade. The word *must* is one of the curses with which Mankind is baptized. The saying: "It must needs be that offenses come; but woe to him by whom the offense cometh" is terrifying. What is it in us that lies, murders, steals? I no longer care to pursue this thought.

Here in brief is the core of *Danton's Death*. In fact, the same phrases occur in the play itself and reappear later in various forms in the other works. They served as inflexible guideposts for the remaining few years of his tragic life.

What precisely was it in this period of the French Revolution which most caught his attention? It was obviously the character of Georges Danton. The question here is not whether and to what extent Büchner remained faithful to his historical characters. The primary consideration is what they are in the play. In several instances Büchner defied history in so far as his characters are concerned, though they do conform to the over-all prospect he had of the historical period. And indeed he made his *Danton* characters reflections of that age, and in the figure of Georges Danton its proponent. Danton, indeed, is not merely the philosophical center of the play, he is as close as any dramatic author has ever come to putting himself into his own work. Almost every speech of Danton's can be traced to Büchner's letters or other personal statements. Danton is even endowed with his author's own ambivalence of attitude, a minor consideration, to be sure, but one no less significant for that.

Danton's Death has been severely criticized for the fact that it is a static play, that Danton is virtually nonexistent as a dramatic character in that he performs not a single plot-progressing action, that he is the most undramatic character ever conceived of by a playwright, that the play lacks any personal contact or exchange between characters. And every word of this indictment is true, true to the point of being painful—yet at the same time these very characteristics for which it is criticized are among the qualities that make the play something genuinely extraordinary.

Büchner was so much an artist, even at the time of the writing of *Danton*, that he knew one of the first precepts of art is not to force a plot or idea into an existing, acceptable, well-tried, and established form. If a work of art, and especially a literary work, and even more specifically a dramatic composition (lyric poetry and great drama being one) is even to approach perfection, then its form must be dictated by its content, the former must grow inevitably out of the latter. Aristotle said as much; and if I read him correctly he would have happily accepted Büchner's own version of tragedy, just as he would not have quarreled with Arthur Miller, for Woyzeck is the great-grandfather of Willy Loman.

Few works in the history of drama are so much a union of form and content as *Danton's Death*. This is true to the point of perhaps being a fault. Danton as the central figure is motivated by nothing: he is stationary, static, from the standpoint of action; he has one desire, an overwhelming longing for death as a result of disillusionment and ultimate boredom. It would be superfluous to remark that he is not the most ideal of central characters. And yet he is a most intriguing one.

What is it that makes him so? If not action, then something else. The answer lies in the convenient title we must tab him with: *Passive Hero*. Strangely enough, he *is* a hero, pathetic, to be sure, but hero nonetheless. And this pathos springs from his attitude of mind, his—what shall we call it?—universal anguish. He is the only one in the entire play (save for his young comrade Camille, who has premonitions of it) who fully and tragically comprehends the human condition. Yes, Danton is a hero; not because he *does*, but because he *would do* if he knew that his doing would have any efficacy whatever. But life and all life's actions are futile, doomed to destruction, without meaning or reason Each man exists in himself and is unable to break that impenetrable shell. Man is isolated. He knows no real communication with his fellow men. He is adrift on a sea of impersonal blindness. It was probably in February 1834 that Büchner wrote to his fiancée the following:

How eager I am for a letter from you! I am alone as though in the grave; when will your message waken me? My friends desert me, we scream in one another's ears as though deaf; I wish we were dumb, then we could only look at one another—recently I have scarcely been able to look one in the eyes except tears come.

Yet only Danton in the play is aware of this situation; the others *do*, they *act*, or *think they act*, blind to the fact, as Danton is not, that we are dragged along by the relentlessness of Fate or History, or call it what we will. We are crushed beneath it, as Büchner says in his letter. It is this knowledge on Danton's part that constitutes the greater part of his tragic condition. Were it not for this vision of the abyss which Danton must peer into and shudder at, he too would act. He acted once—but in the past; he was responsible for the September Massacre, the tenth of August, and the thirty-first of May—but then apparently he was naive in the ways of destiny. What possible reason has he to act now? His anguish is so great, as well as his desire to communicate, to experience real love and friendship, that we must see some part of him in his vision of the universal force (be it what it may be) when he says to himself on the night preceding his death on the guillotine:

The stars are scattered through the night like glistening teardrops; what a terrible grief must be behind the eyes that dropped them.

Danton no more believes in God than did Büchner, yet he seems to imply that if there were God, how great His anguish and grief would have to be as He looked down on His bungled work, seeing the misery, the suffering and pain, to which His incompetent universal Artificer's craft gave being. But God does not exist, says Büchner in his play; if He did He could not endure the senseless pain and suffering to which Man is subject. Pain, then, is the foremost proof of the nonexistence of God. And if there is no God, then there is nothing to which to cling, there is no recourse. Woyzeck says it: "When God goes, everything goes."

> It is said [writes Büchner in February 1834] I am a ridiculer. True, I laugh a great deal; but my laughter is not at *how* a human being is, but rather at the fact *that* he is a human being; about which he can do nothing; and at the same time I laugh at myself because I must share in his fate.

This might have come from Danton, because in his reasoned passivity he surely sees the pitiable ludicrousness of the human condition.

Despite all this, both Büchner and Danton have an innate ambivalence. Büchner wrote to his parents: "It is my opinion that if anything in our time can help us, then it is force." And later:

> I will of course act moderately in regard to my principles, yet I have learned in recent years that only the urgent need of the majority is capable of bringing about change, and that all the excitement and screaming of individuals is only the idle work of fools. They write—but no one reads them; they cry out—but no one hears; they act—but no one helps them.

And still later he wrote that he refrains from revolutionary activity neither because of scorn nor fear, but because at the time he regards every revolutionary movement as a vain enterprise.

And through the figure of Danton he says that force is ineffectual, and to act, futile. Yet Danton says in the prison scene just before his death that he and his friends may die, but it is possible that their bones, washed up by the flood of the Revolution, will be picked up by the people and be used to bash in the heads of the kings. A strangely optimistic note for Danton.

This duality makes him a most interesting character. At times he seems to himself two persons, each one different from the other. It is this facet which gives him greater interest and depth; it creates a tension, a mental struggle inside him, as when, after longing for death, he believes for a single moment that he would rather live despite life's torments, because not even death is desirable: death is not peace, not nothingness; even in death every atom of him would exist in torment. But again this duality is one of the mind; it never culminates in action.

Paradoxically, this Danton, the passive hero, is surrounded by much confusion and bustle, by crowd scenes and violence (the background rather than the substance of legitimate dramatic action), by people like Robespierre and his followers who believe their words communicate, but who only mouth empty and impersonal and formalistic oratory and rhetoric. As Lee Baxandall has recently pointed out, the characters of *Danton's Death* do not speak *to*, but *past* one another; they speak not to elicit reply, but to convince; not even what has been called the "monologic lyricism" of Danton and of his followers is spoken to elicit reply. The most extreme example of this is the final "Conciergerie" scene which is scarcely more than a great fugal hymn to Nihilism, certainly one of the finest, though least dramatic, sections of the play. Such dialogue cannot be dramatic. It is instructive to read through the play omitting all speeches save those of Danton. Virtually every one is a philosophical comment or reminiscence of past actions, a descant on existing circumstances, the laments of a tormented mind. And yet the anguish in these statements, the bitterness, the pathos of them, makes Danton a truly remarkable figure. He *lives* his thoughts. He has made of his life the mirror of his mind. And so has Büchner made the form of his play the mirror of its philosophical core: form and content are successfully one, almost to the point of being a fault—and yet what an admirable fault it is.

In the event that it comes to your hands [wrote Büchner to his parents concerning the first, mutilated, publication of *Danton's Death*], I beg you to consider, before you judge it, that I was compelled to be true to History and to show the men of the Revolution as they were; bloodthirsty, dissolute, vigorous, and cynical. I regard my play as an historical painting, which must be like its original. . . .

He was concerned with the crudities of language, of course; but he was more concerned with not covering over the real men and their motives with false idealism in the manner of a Schiller. It did not matter how terrible or embarrassing the picture presented, if only it was true. About *Danton's Death* Büchner wrote the following to Karl Gutzkow:

What I am to make of it myself, I do not know, except for this, that I have every cause to grow red with shame where History is concerned; nonetheless, I console myself with the thought that, except for Shakespeare, all poets stand as schoolboys before History and Nature.

On July 28, 1835, he set down in a letter to his parents what must be regarded as one of the most impressive and impeccable theories of dramatic art ever formulated. It is all the more remarkable considering the date of its composition, some fifty-four years before the official beginning of German Naturalism, the first performance of Gerhart Hauptmann's *Before Sunrise,* and fifty-six years prior to Hauptmann's *Weavers,* which might not have existed had it not been for the example of *Danton's Death.* And now, another half-century after the decline of Naturalism, Büchner's dictum concerning truth and the artist in relation to Nature is with us again in the guise of the New Drama, the Theatre of the Absurd.

In 1835 Büchner wrote:

The dramatic poet is, in my eyes, nothing but a writer of history, except that he stands above the latter in that he creates history for the second time; he transplants us directly into the life of another time, instead of giving us a dry account of it; instead of characteristics, he gives us characters; instead of descriptions, he gives us living figures. His greatest task is to come as close as possible to history as it actually was. His book may be neither more nor less moral than history itself; but history was not made by the Good Lord God to serve as proper reading matter for young ladies, and therefore I ought not to be blamed if my drama happens to be equally unsuited to that purpose. I can scarcely be expected to make virtuous heroes out of Danton and the bandits of the Revolution! If I was to depict their dissoluteness then I had to make them dissolute; if I was to show them as Godless then I had to let them speak like atheists. If a number of indecent expressions present themselves, then consider the well-known obscenity utilized in the speech of the time, and you will see that that which I have let my people say is no more than a weak abstract of it. I might still, of course, be censured for having chosen such material. But that objection was put down long ago. If one were to put it into effect, then it would be necessary to repudiate the greatest masterworks of literature. The poet is no teacher of morals; he invents and creates characters, he brings the past back to life, and from this people may learn as though from the study of history itself and the observation of it, what happens in human life around them. If one objects to this reasoning, then he ought not to study history at all because a great many immoral things happen therein; he should have to go blindfold down the street, for he might otherwise be compelled to see certain indecencies; he should have to cry shame on God for having created a world which gives rise to so much dissoluteness. Furthermore, if someone should say to me that the poet ought not to show the world as it is, but as it ought to be, then I would answer him that I will not make it better than the Good Lord, who must certainly have made it as it ought to be. As regards those so-called Idealist poets, I find that they have given us nothing more than marionettes with sky-blue noses and affected pathos, but not human beings of flesh and blood, who make us feel their joy and sorrow with them, and whose deeds and actions fill me with revulsion or admiration. In a word, I have great fondness for Goethe or Shakespeare, but very little for Schiller.

What there is of Schiller and Idealism in Büchner's work is parody, as in the high-flown language and declamation of the Simon scenes. From Goethe and Shakespeare he received truth and suggestions concerning form, but in the last analysis he transformed what he acquired into something wholly his own. *Danton* reminds one of *Götz* and Shakespeare's Roman plays, especially *Antony and Cleopatra* and *Coriolanus*. His fitful changes of scene may seem unnecessary, yet they are highly significant as regards his design and intention. What at first may seem chaotic and arbitrary actually achieves almost breathtaking relevance. Büchner's shrewd juxtaposition of scenes in *Danton* (so much a part of his theory of fidelity to Nature) evokes a mosaiclike pattern of restlessness and indecision. "The Open Field" scene in which Danton is almost flippant about his impending arrest is followed by "A Room. Night," in which he is tormented by memory and conscience, and doubts the validity of his former actions. It is the sort of scene with which Büchner punctuates his work. These moments are brief and fleeting, as in life itself, but they are the more poignant for that fact: their brevity points up their fragility. They are moments in which poetry and horror are firmly bound up with one another; moments in which we are shown the terrifying abyss which threatened Danton and Büchner.

Then suddenly, as though a knife had severed the fragile thread which balances one between life and the abyss, the scene changes rapidly to the "Street in Front of Danton's House," with its Shakespearean buffoonery, its parody of the "How goes the night" scene in Macbeth, and of Ancient Pistol's going off to the wars, as well as other typical Büchner crudities. To call such an arrangement chaos or even disorderly is to call *Antony*, that extreme example of Shakespeare's theatrical genius in the art of scenic arrangement, formless and confused. In *Danton's Death* Büchner is literally holding the mirror up to Nature, and in so doing he is fulfilling the precepts of his own dramatic theory.

Leonce and Lena

What is it in *Leonce and Lena* that causes it to be so often dismissed by critics and producers? It may, of course, be less in stature than either *Danton's Death* or *Woyzeck*, but it is not what too many of Büchner's critics claim it to be, an unoriginal work. Relatively speaking, perhaps; but this ought not to be held against it. The play has been described as wholesale literary borrowing, as being a direct descendant of the *commedia dell'arte* tradition, as being weak in having caricatures rather than characters. In a sense each of these accusations is true. And yet each of them may have been intended by the author. The fact that it was written as an entry in a drama contest sponsored by a Stuttgart publisher, and that a comedy was needed, is of little significance.

If the play is more lightly passed over than the other works, it is because it is not so easily understandable, it is elusive, deceptive. Furthermore, it shows us a side of Büchner that is not so fully developed in *Danton* and *Woyzeck*. This side is simply that Büchner, for all his complaints against Schiller and Romanticism and Idealism, and his insistence on Naturalism, is nonetheless a Romantic. The important thing is that he is not what one would call a German Romanticist. A. H. J. Knight defined Büchner's position rather well when he said that he is unsentimental, but not unemotional or unromantic. Still, his Romantic elements are not those of Schiller and his school; they are straightforward and uncluttering. Where in *Leonce and Lena* he may seem to be following German Romanticism he is merely exaggerating so as to parody and consequently make nonsense of it. Again Knight would seem to be correct when he isolates this as a Heine-like element, and asserts that it is neither Romantic nor of the Young German Movement, but one of the play's most original elements.

Yes, *Leonce* is derivative. Its philosophical allusions are seemingly endless, its debts to Musset's *Fantasio*, to the image of Sancho Panza, to the monologues, as Hans Mayer points out, of Manfred, Childe Harold, and Don Juan, and to the tirades of the heroes of Tieck and Brentano, are obvious—but there is more to *Leonce and Lena* than this. It is as much a part of Büchner's work and thought as either *Danton* or *Woyzeck*. It is permeated with the same bitterness, even though this is seemingly softened by the so-called comic vision. *Leonce* is a severe attack on most of the injustices and stupidities prevalent in the Germany of Büchner's time. It rails against typical German Romanticism and its consequent ennui; it attacks Idealism; it is a diatribe against the sameness of the formalistic life; and finally, it is infused with the bitter fatalism of History, except that its characters *do* act, unlike Danton, because they do not realize their predicament; they exert what they wrongly take to be their free will. Both Leonce and Lena flee their separate kingdoms so as to avoid the preordained marriage to one another, even though they have never met. Still, they *do* meet, unknown to each other, fall in love, are married, ironically as proxies for the actual prince and princess, which is to say by Fate, and only then discover to their chagrin the truth of the matter.

All this is a gentler version of Danton's vision of the wild horse of the world set loose, dragging him with it, helpless, across the abyss. For all its dream-world atmosphere, *Leonce and Lena* is as real a world beneath its surface as *Danton* and *Woyzeck*, because this dream world is forever being intruded upon by the harshness and cruelty of pessimism and fatalism. The ironic apotheosis of this comic vision of the abyss comes during the two final speeches of the play. All having turned out "happily," Leonce says:

And so, Lena, you see how our pockets are stuffed with puppets and playthings. What shall we do with them? Shall we make mustaches for them and hang broadswords about their waists? Or shall we dress them in frockcoats and let them practice infusorial politics and diplomacy, and sit here watching them through our microscopes? Or would you prefer a barrel-organ on which milk-white esthetic shrews flit about? Shall we build a theatre? [LENA *leans against him, shakes her head.*] Oh, but I know what it is you really want: we shall have all the clocks in the kingdom destroyed, forbid all calendars, and count off hours and months with the chronometer of the flowers, according to times of planting and times of harvest. And then we shall surround our tiny kingdom with burning glasses so that winter no longer exists, and in summer we shall rise up through a process of distillation as high as Ischia and Capri, and all year long live amidst roses and violets, surrounded with orange and laurel boughs.

And Valerio:

And I'll be the Minister of State, and I'll issue a decree which reads: that anyone who works calluses on his hands will be placed in custody of a guardian; that anyone who works himself sick will be criminally prosecuted; that every man who prides himself on eating bread earned in the sweat of his brow will be declared insane and a hazard to human society. And then we shall lie in the shade and ask the Lord God for macaroni, melons, and figs, for voices soft as music, for bodies fine as classical heroes, and for a commodious religion!

Woyzeck

What is it that constitutes Büchner's modernity almost a century and a quarter after his death, and that assures him an indisputable place in world literature? The answer lies deeper than his artistry; it has to do with more than the manner of his dialogue, the juxtaposition of his scenes, his delineation of character. The core of the matter lies in the scientific clarity of his vision and of his unfailing concern with the estate of Man.

Woyzeck is the first modern tragedy. It is the first *wholly* successful tragic representation of the common man

on the stage, a representation which shows him capable of
greatness of mind and soul and feeling, except he is
kept from the realization of this by the millstone of
environment hung about his neck.

Woyzeck is the great precursor of the Naturalist Movement, and its effect is with us again today in the Theatre
of the Absurd. As a drama of social criticism Woyzeck
has never been, and very likely never will be, superseded.
Its power lies in the fact that its problems are, in addition
to being specific, universal in time and place. Yet more
is required of a great work than that it be an exposé of
misery and social injustice. This may be the ultimate
downfall of most of the works that constitute the Theatre
of the Absurd. For all their bitterness and social indignation, the greater number of these plays lack a vision of
life that can serve as an apotheosis, that can transform
them into works of the heart rather than of the groin.
They lack an implicit moral center based on empirical
evidence. The feeling that there might be such a center is
always evident in Büchner. To write a sordid drama with
social implications is only the first step. The apotheosis
comes as a result of profound and overwhelming understanding of, and sympathy with, the estate of Man, with
his suffering and struggle.

The basis of Büchner's vision is precisely that upon
which the Theatre of the Absurd is founded. It is simply
that the Absurd is that which is without purpose, futile,
out of harmony with its surroundings. In short, the human
condition is senseless. One play among all the modern
works comes readily to mind, Beckett's Waiting for
Godot. It is the logical successor to Büchner's vision. Its
manner may be different on the surface, but its attitudes
are one with Büchner's. Passivity is the universal disease.
Man waits and waits (that is, if he has even only a
remnant of hope) but nothing comes. Man acts, or thinks
he acts, but all is futile. In Godot there is also greatness
of mind, though not in the degree that we find it in
Büchner, and this overwhelming sympathy with Man.

In both these plays this sympathy is never expressed,
it is implict. In Godot it is implied in the pathos en-
gendered by the unrelenting sameness of life. In Woyzeck

the method is different. In essence, Büchner's method in *Woyzeck* and *Danton* is the same: juxtaposition of scenes. (We may reasonably assume this, despite the fact that Büchner left the scenes of *Woyzeck* unarranged at his death.) As in the Epic Theatre of Brecht, who owes his greatest debt to Büchner, each scene is virtually autonomous, yet when assembled they constitute a seemingly indissoluble whole. Each scene works with the others and comments implicitly upon them. Thus we understand the reasons for Woyzeck's state of mind and body, for his hallucinations, when we see him literally turned into a guinea pig by the Doctor's scientific observations and his injunction to eat "nothing but peas," as well as by the Captain's interminable prodding about his strangeness and his inability to keep Marie faithful to him.

Less a mosaic in structure than *Danton*, *Woyzeck* is more akin to a series of stained-glass windows in a medieval cathedral. In logical sequence one representation after another (each a self-contained unity) succeeds in telling the whole story. *Danton*, on the other hand, is more a gigantic panorama—a mosaic panorama, to be sure, since its individual pieces are not always inevitably positioned—which seems to show the whole story at a glance. *Danton* can be thought of *only* as a whole, *Woyzeck* both in that way and as individual scenes. In this way it is more akin to Epic Theatre than *Danton*.

The chief virtue of *Woyzeck's* structure lies in its simplicity of development, in the uncluttered vision and lack of Germanic ponderousness. *Woyzeck* is clearly the product of a scientific mind. It is as dispassionate in any explicit way as a medical lecture. This clarity and sharpness of focus are due in great part to Büchner's practice of fully developing only his major character or characters. Only Woyzeck and Marie are fully rounded individuals. The others are boldly, succinctly, and incisively drawn, but they are shown in only one attitude. Woyzeck and Marie are seen in a whole range of attitudes; they are given to thinking about their state and condition, and to suffering pangs of conscience and despair. The others are utilized to set them off, to illustrate them in a gamut of situations. The fact that they are typical inventions may be seen in their being called simply Doctor, Captain, Drum Major, etc. They are there to *use* Woyzeck for their own ends; in short, to make a virtual animal of him, to point up the fact that Woyzeck in order to exist *must* hand himself over as a guinea pig to society. A properly organized society would not give rise to such a condition. If Woyzeck is to live, then he *must* do as he is *forced* to do by economic necessity. Büchner was one of the first to bring attention to the economic factor in society. When the Captain lectures him on virtue and morals, Woyzeck retorts:

Yes, Captain, sir: Virtue. I haven't got much of that. You see, us common people, we haven't got virtue. That's the way it's got to be. But if I could be a gentleman, and if I could have a hat and a watch and a cane, and if I could talk refined, I'd want to be virtuous, all right. There must be something beautiful in virtue, Captain, sir.

And on the subject of morals:

You see, Captain, sir . . . Money, money! Whoever hasn't got money . . . Well, who's got morals when he's bringing something like me into the world? We're flesh and blood, too. Our kind is miserable only once: in this world and in the next. I think if we ever got to Heaven we'd have to help with the thunder.

Danton asks that often-repeated question in Büchner's thought; it is the question to the answer which Woyzeck gives above. Asks Danton: "What is this in us that lies, whores, steals, and murders?" In the great metaphor which *Woyzeck* is, Büchner seems to answer: Society, Environment, Circumstance. And Danton says:

What are we but puppets, manipulated on wires by unknown powers? We are nothing, nothing in ourselves: we are the swords that spirits fight with—except no one sees the hands— just as in fairy tales. . . .

Lenz and The Hessian Courier

The composition of the *Lenz* fragment is positioned between the completion of *Danton's Death* and *Leonce and Lena*, and comprises Büchner's sole effort in the realm of nondramatic narrative prose. It is assumed that

Lenz was to be a novel and that Büchner was never able to finish it, and yet it is relatively complete in itself as a picture of one segment in the life of the historical Jacob Michael Reinhold Lenz, born in 1751 in Livonia, who became an acquaintance of Goethe's, was known for his highly eccentric behavior, and finally died in obscurity, some say a beggar, near Moscow in 1792.

Lenz is by all standards one of the most remarkable pieces of German narrative prose ever composed. Its narrative style constitutes a category all its own, with its strange repetitions, its colloquial expressions, and its often maddening compressions.

The events of the piece were based on fact, having been drawn (often almost word for word) from Oberlin's diary, which came to Büchner's attention in October 1835. He wrote to his parents from Strasbourg:

I have obtained all sorts of interesting notes concerning a friend of Goethe's, an unhappy poet named Lenz, who lived here at the time of Goethe and became somewhat mad. I am considering writing an article about it for the *Deutsches Revue.*

In addition to its eccentric and vigorous prose style (which, as in *Danton,* seems to be a perfect marriage of form and content), *Lenz* is also important for its long section devoted to a theory of art. Stephen Spender has pointed out that Büchner adapted the theory from Lenz's own writings. It seems valid, however, to accept it as Büchner's own, formulated, perhaps, under the influence of Lenz, for we find in that section ideas as well as phrases which turn up again and again in Büchner's work. The central idea is that art must remain faithful to nature. Lenz attacks Idealism and Romanticism with a bitterness worthy and characteristic of Büchner. God, he says, did not create the world only to have Man re-create it and try to make it better than it is.

Let them [says Lenz, speaking of Idealist writers] try just once to immerse themselves in the life of humble people and then reproduce this again in all its movements, its implications, in its subtle, scarcely discernible play of expression . . .

Lenz's theory of Beauty is equally interesting and important in the light it throws on Büchner's own work.

Lenz describes a walk into the mountains where he saw two girls seated on a rock, the one binding up her hair, the other helping her. It was so beautiful a picture that he wished to be able to preserve it by turning it into stone and calling the world to see it. But then—and this is the significant point—they rose and the picture dissolved, "the beautiful grouping was destroyed; but as they descended between the rocks they formed another picture." Lenz continues:

The most beautiful pictures, the most swelling tones, form a group and then dissolve. Only one thing remains: an unending beauty which passes from one form to another, eternally revealed, eternally unchanged.

One has only to read through *Lenz* to see the application of this theory. One sees it, too, in the dramas, in the sudden coming together of events and characters which constitute moments, however brief, of extraordinary poignancy, only to dissolve again as quickly and as effortlessly as they formed, attesting, as it were, to the durable and indestructible fragility of Beauty.

The descriptions in *Lenz* are wholly Büchner's own. So much so, in fact, that the description of Lenz's passage through the mountains is a direct recollection of an excursion made by Büchner into the Vosges and celebrated in a letter to his family in the spring of 1833, at least two years before he discovered the *Lenz* material in Oberlin's diary. There are other parts of *Lenz* which call to mind sections of *Danton's Death*, particularly the pessimism expressed through Paine in the prison scene, the impeachment of God from the standpoint of the pain and suffering to which Man is subject. The closing paragraph of *Lenz* reminds one of portions, especially images, in the then still-to-be-written *Leonce and Lena*.

If *Lenz* is a fragment of a projected longer work, I think it is not wholly wrong to suppose that Büchner, had he had the time to complete the work, would not have chosen to do so. The work is too eccentric, too intense, too impulsive, to have been carried to completion. As it stands now, its greatness and integrity strain the sensibilities of the reader. Perhaps Büchner realized that, too. Perhaps

he felt that he was incapable of providing sufficient variety
to render the projected work acceptable. Nonetheless, we
must be grateful for even this small segment, which has
exerted its own influence on succeeding generations of
great German prose stylists.

Of *The Hessian Courier* there is little to say except that
it is the first extended effort of the young socialist revolutionary. It can scarcely be regarded as a literary work
in its own right, and yet it is not entirely devoid of such
distinction. Its principal importance is to help the reader
complete the portrait of Büchner which his works provide, especially since it is impossible to understand the
man fully without an awareness of his political sympa-
thies.

The Hessian Courier shows the work of a young, bitter,
rebellious, and still naive, genius. It is obviously the product of his research into the French Revolution of 1789,
which a year after *The Hessian Courier* gave rise to
Danton's Death. In this work, a semisocialistic political
pamphlet written and circulated in 1834, we find Büchner,
intensely influenced by the Revolution, advocating a
thoroughgoing revolt by the German people to overthrow
their ruling class, their princes, their governmental institutions, everything, in order to help themselves to the
freedom which is their right. He points out to them
the mistakes made by the populace in the French Revolution and exhorts them against running aground in the
same manner. His vision of Revolution, however, was
still somewhat too naive to be practicable. Nonetheless,
the pamphlet remains one of the most impressive political
documents ever written, mainly by virtue of the passion
and bitter sarcasm which are so much a part of it. It also
gives some inkling of the writer still to come.

Conclusions

Büchner's intense and lifelong searching led only to
nothingness, senselessness, and futility. History, morality,
the arbitrary and needless course of events, were all with-

out the slightest particle of meaning. He came to one conclusion: that Man is dirt, sand, and dung; this was for him the sole certainty. Had he lived to maturity he might well have transcended the entire body of German dramatists and drama, and his influence might have been even greater, if that were possible. At any rate it would have exerted itself far sooner than half a century after his death. Yet his pessimism, his determinism, his incurable sense of the futility and senselessness of the universe, however sincerely he might have searched, would only have deepened his belief in his conclusions and would have embittered him all the more, only to make of him as tragic a figure as the history of drama can boast of having nurtured.

The fact is, however, that he did *not* look for God, because he *knew* He could not exist; and if He were possible Büchner would only have challenged Him, as one critic has so aptly put it, to justify His brutality, His indifference, His invariable inhumanity toward Man.

Büchner was no fool. He could not postulate a God and proceed from there as so many others have done. He had to assume that God *is not* until he found Him. But, then, he knew the search was futile. It was not merely the senselessness and futility, the lack of direction and purpose in the world, that told him there is no God, or if there were then that He is a bungler; rather, the existence of pain, of suffering, was the only proof he needed to cement his convictions.

Consider this, Anaxagoras [says Paine in *Danton's Death*]: Why do I suffer? That is the very bedrock of atheism. The least quiver of pain, in even the smallest of atoms, makes a rent in the curtain of your creation from top to bottom.

And again:

One can deny evil, but not pain; only reasoning can prove God, feeling rebels against it.

Büchner's plays are a living testimonial to his life. And yet it is reported that in his last illness, shortly before death overtook him, he said:

There is not too much suffering in our lives, there is too little, for it is through suffering that we reach God. We are death, dust, ashes, how should we complain?

A curious end to an even more curious life.

CARL RICHARD MUELLER
University of California, Los Angeles
All Saints' Day, 1962

A NOTE ON THE TEXTS

Except for *Woyzeck*, the texts of the plays contained in this volume are relatively stable. *Woyzeck*, however, was left in a state of confusion and incompleteness at the time of Büchner's death. Consequently many editions of the work vary according to the opinions of individual editors. The conventionally edited form of *Woyzeck* is reasonably well known to English-speaking readers through other translations. However, what many readers are unaware of is that there exist many entire scenes and fragments of scenes in Bergemann's major critical edition of Büchner in German which have never been incorporated into the actual body of the play. Many of these pieces are early versions of scenes; others are wholly new. Since any editing of the text is arbitrary according to the viewpoint of the editor or editor-translator, and since the so-to-speak discarded scenes contain much good and original material, I have decided to make what to my knowledge is an entirely new version of the play. I have utilized all scenes which I felt could legitimately be placed within the confines of the conventionally edited text, and I have eliminated nothing of that text. In a number of instances I have lifted from discarded scenes, the whole of which could not be used, small segments, at times only a sentence, and grafted them into the established scenes. My intention has been simply to amplify the conventional text wherever possible, that is, without violating Büchner's design, or what I take it to have been. I have mainly added to the character of Woyzeck, and as a consequence he is a somewhat different person, certainly a fuller one, a being, at least to my mind, more in keeping with Büchner's whole range of thought than the Woyzeck we have known up to the present. One small, though significant, change is in the ending of the play. Generally Woyzeck dies in the pond while washing himself of the blood. Yet there is every indication that Büchner meant to bring Woyzeck back from the pond (witness the scene when he comes in to embrace his child and is dripping wet). Büchner, I feel, would have completed the play by showing the absolute and inhuman destruction of his main character by means of as ghastly a trial as he could possibly have devised, a veritable travesty of justice (much in the style of the trial scenes in a number of Brecht plays). It would have been a fitting end to this most horrifying and modern of dramas. I feel there is no violation in bringing Woyzeck back from the pond; the scene, after all, is Büchner's. I have, however, discarded a scene which is not Büchner's but a convenient merger of various scenes by his first editor, Karl Emil Franzos. No line of this new version is my own. The sole "unauthorized" addition is found in the stage direction to the final scene. I have added a number of persons not called for by Büchner. I felt it necessary that the chief persons in Woyzeck's case be present in order to heighten the irony necessary to make the scene as terrifying and coldly inhuman as possible. The audience must sense the terrors which await Woyzeck at his trial. It must be implicit in the situation, in the grouping, and, in short, in everything else which the imaginative director may legitimately be able to devise.

I should like to warn prospective directors against the use of the music from the operatic version of the play by Alban Berg. Without doubt it is one of the high-water marks of modern operatic literature and is a work impeccable in its own right. Yet to use its music in a dramatic production does not illuminate Büchner's play. To use it is to be ignorant of the true nature of his work. Büchner, from his earliest times, was nurtured on the folk music of his native Germany, and *Woyzeck* is in every way a manifestation of that early love for folk music instilled in the young Büchner by his mother. In a letter written by the young student to his fiancée, he asks her to sing him some of the old songs when he sees her again. To see *Woyzeck* correctly, then, is to see it as a dramatic folk song. It should be a clue to the type of music the play demands. In every instance the music must be simplicity through and through, for the play is nothing but simplicity, and to violate that is to destroy it.

Finally, I have omitted those parts of *The Hessian Courier* which are generally recognized as interpolations into Büchner's text by Friedrich Ludwig Weidig, teacher, rector, defender of liberalism and German unification, and writer of anonymous political pamphlets. His amplifications in *The Hessian Courier* are not only unnecessary, they serve to distort Büchner's original with their fanatical ravings and protestations in the manner of a nineteenth century Jeremiah.

Georg Büchner
COMPLETE PLAYS AND PROSE

DANTON'S DEATH

A *Drama*

CHARACTERS

Deputies of the National Convention
GEORGES DANTON
LEGENDRE
CAMILLE DESMOULINS
HÉRAULT-SÉCHELLES
LACROIX
PHILIPPEAU
FABRE D'EGLANTINE
MERCIER
THOMAS PAINE

 Members of the Committee of Public Safety
ROBESPIERRE
SAINT-JUST
BARÈRE
COLLOT D'HERBOIS
BILLAUD-VARENNES

 Members of the Committee of General Security
AMAR
VOULAND

 Presidents of the Revolutionary Tribunal
HERMAN
DUMAS
CHAUMETTE, *Procurator of the Commune*

DILLON, *a General*
FOUQUIER-TINVILLE, *Public Prosecutor*
PARIS, *a friend of Danton's*
SIMON, *a theatrical prompter*
SIMON'S WIFE
LAFLOTTE
JULIE, *Danton's wife*
LUCILLE, *Camille Desmoulins' wife*
ROSALIE, *a whore*
ADELAIDE, *a whore*
MARION, *a whore*

Ladies at gaming tables, ladies and gentlemen together with a young gentleman and Eugénie on a promenade, citizens, citizen-soldiers, deputies from Lyons, other deputies, Jacobins, presidents of the Jacobin Club and the National Convention, jailers, executioners, and carters, men and women of the people, whores, ballad-singer, beggar, etc.

DANTON'S DEATH

ACT ONE

SCENE 1—A drawing room

HÉRAULT-SÉCHELLES *and some ladies at a gaming table.*
DANTON *and* JULIE, *somewhat farther off,* DANTON *on a*
stool at JULIE's *feet.*

DANTON. Look at that sweet little bitch over there! She
knows how to play her cards all right; deals her husband
the hearts and every other man her——. You women
could make *any* man fall in love with a lie.

Julie. Danton, do you believe in me?

Danton. How should I know! We know little enough
about one another. We're thick-skinned creatures who
reach out our hands toward one another, but it means
nothing—leather rubbing against leather—we're very
lonely.

Julie. But you know me, Danton.

Danton. Yes, that's what they call it. You have dark
eyes and curly hair and a delicate complexion and you
always call me: dear Georges! But [*Touches her forehead*
and eyelids.] what about here, and here? What goes on
behind here? No, there's nothing delicate about our
senses. Know one another? We'd have to crack open our
skulls and drag each other's thoughts out by the tails.

Lady [*to* HÉRAULT-SÉCHELLES]. Just what is it you have
in mind there with your fingers?

Hérault-Séchelles. Why, nothing!

Lady. Then don't crook your thumbs in that way, I can't
stand the sight of it!

Hérault-Séchelles. Understand, my love, such things
can't be put down simply by willing.

Danton. No, Julie, I love you as I love the grave.

Julie [*turning away*]. Oh!

Danton. No, listen to me! They say that there's peace

3

in the grave, and that grave and peace are one. If that is true, then whenever I lie with you I already lie beneath the earth. O you precious grave, your lips are passing bells, your voice their knell, your breasts my burial mound and your heart my coffin.

Lady. You lose!

Hérault-Séchelles. Well, amorous adventures cost money the same as all the others.

Lady. You declare your love like a deaf-mute—on your fingers.

Hérault-Séchelles. And why not? One might say that they are less likely to be misunderstood. I arranged an affair with a queen, my fingers were princes transformed into spiders, and you, madame, were the Good Fairy. But it didn't work out too well: the queen was always in childbed whelping sixty knaves a minute. I'll never let a daughter of mine play a game like that: all these ladies and gentlemen playing at goats and monkeys and the knave coming so soon after.

CAMILLE DESMOULINS *and* PHILIPPEAU *enter.*

Hérault-Séchelles. Philippeau, how sad you look! Did you tear a hole in your red cap? Has Saint Jacob made a nasty face at you? Did it rain while they were guillotining this morning? Oh—and you got a bad seat and couldn't see a thing!

Camille. Parodying Socrates perhaps? Do you know what that most excellent of philosophers said one day to Alcibiades when he saw him sad and depressed? "Did you lose your shield on the battlefield?" he said. "Were you beaten in a race or at sword-fighting? Did someone sing or play the lyre better than you?" There was a classical republican for you! We ought to exchange some of our guillotine Romanticism for that!

Philippeau. Another twenty victims fell today. We were wrong: the only reason the Hébertists were sent to the scaffold was that they weren't systematic enough, and perhaps, too, because the Decemvirs thought themselves lost if any man should last a whole week and be more feared than they.

Hérault-Séchelles. They'd like to send us back to the

Stone Age. Saint-Just would be pleased if we crawled around on all fours again; that way Robespierre could invent for us, according to the instructions of our good Monsieur Rousseau, the watchmaker's son from Geneva, all sorts of caps and school benches and an Almighty God.

Philippeau. They would never hesitate to add a few more zeros to Marat's death figures. How much longer must we be base and bloody as newborn children, with coffins for cradles, and play with heads? We must make some advance: the Committee of Clemency for Prisoners must be put into effect and the expelled deputies reinstated!

Hérault-Séchelles. The Revolution must be reorganized. The Revolution must end and the Republic begin. In our Constitution we must place right above duty, contentment above virtue, and self-preservation above punishment. Every man must assert himself and be able to live according to his own nature. He can be reasonable or unreasonable, educated or ignorant, good or bad—that has nothing to do with the state. We're all fools, and not one of us has the right to impose his own foolishness on anyone else. Every man must be able to find pleasure in his own way, but only in so far as he does not do so at another's expense or disturb another's pleasure.

Camille. The Constitution must be a transparent veil that clings close to the body of the people. Through it we must see the pulsing of each vein, the flexing of every muscle, the quiver of every sinew. Her body can be beautiful or ugly, because it has the right to be exactly what it is; and we have no right to dress her as we see fit. We shall rap the knuckles of them who see fit to cast nun's veils across the naked shoulders of our sinful but beloved France. We want our gods to be naked and our goddesses to be free with themselves. Olympian delights and lips that sing melodiously of wicked love that sets the body free! We would never think of preventing our good Roman Robespierre and his virtuous Republicans from cooking their carrots in a corner, but let them know that there will be no more gladiatorial games. Our most excellent Epicurus and Venus with her delightful buttocks must stand as porters of our Republic in place of Marat and St. Chalier.—Danton, you must lead the attack at the next Convention!

Danton. I must, *you* must, *he* must. If we live that long, as the old women say. In an hour we shall have sixty minutes less to live. Right, my boy?

Desmoulins. What has that to do with it? It stands to reason.

Danton. Yes, everything stands to reason. Who do you propose should set all these grand ideas in motion?

Philippeau. Ourselves and all other honorable people.

Danton. That's a rather large *and* I should say; it puts us at some distance from one another; in fact it's far enough that Honesty will lose her breath before we meet. And what if we do! All that one can do with honorable people is lend them money, be godfather to their children, and marry one's daughters to them!

Camille. If you knew that when you began, why did you ever start to fight?

Danton. Because these followers of Robespierre with their puritanical ways were repugnant to me. Swaggering about like little Catos, I wanted to give them a good boot in the ass. That's the way I am. [*He rises.*]

Julie. You're going?

Danton [*to* JULIE]. I can't stay here. These people and their politics get on my nerves. [*While leaving.*] If I may prophesy hurriedly in passing: our statue of Liberty has not yet been cast, the great furnace is glowing hot, there is still time for us to burn our fingers.   [*Goes off.*

Camille. Leave him alone! Do you really suppose he could keep out of it if it ever came to that?

Hérault-Séchelles. It would only be a pastime with him, like playing chess.

SCENE II—A *street*

SIMON *and his* WIFE.

SIMON [*beating his* WIFE]. You filthy pimp, you haggard poisonous pill, you worm-eaten apple of sin!

Wife. Oh, help me! Help me!

People [*come running*]. Get them apart, get them apart!

Simon. No, leave me be, good Romans! I'll batter her bones to bits! Oh, you holy whore!

Wife. Holy whore! We'll see about that!

Simon.

I'll tear the clothing off your wormy body
And bake your naked carrion in the sun.

O bed of a whore, there's lechery in every wrinkle of your body.

They are separated.

First Citizen. What's the matter?

Simon. Where is the virgin? Tell me! No, I can't call her that. The maiden! No, nor that. That woman, that female! Not that, no, not even that! There's but one single name left—oh, how it chokes me! I have no breath to speak it.

Second Citizen. It's a good thing, too, or it would stink of brandy.

Simon.

O ancient Virginius, veil your hairless head,
The Raven Shame doth sit upon thy pate
And pecks at thine own eyes. A knife, my Romans!

He sinks to the ground.

Wife. He's usually a good man, but he can't take much drink; whisky's a third leg to him.

Second Citizen. Then he walks with three legs.

Wife. No, he falls.

Second Citizen. Of course; first he walks with all three, then falls over the third till the third falls by itself.

Simon. Vampire's tongue! To drink my heart's warm blood!

Wife. Just leave him be, this is about the time he grows sentimental; he'll be all right soon.

First Citizen. What's the matter with him?

Wife. Well, you see, I was sitting on a rock in the sun to warm myself, you see—you see, we've got no wood at home for the fire——

Second Citizen. Try your husband's nose.

Wife. And my daughter went down there around the corner—she's a good girl and supports her parents.

Simon. Ha, she confesses!

8　　　　　　　　GEORG BÜCHNER　　　　[ACT ONE

Wife. You Judas Iscariot! You wouldn't have a pair of pants to pull *up* if those young gentlemen didn't pull theirs *down* with her! You dirty brandy barrel, you want to go thirsty when our little spring dries up? We work with every limb we've got, why not with that one, too? Her mother worked it overtime when she brought her into the world, and it cost her enough pain, too. So why shouldn't *she* work it for her mother! Eh? Even if it does cost her a little pain! Eh? You idiot!

Simon. Ah, Lucretia! A knife, my Romans, give me a knife! O Appius Claudius!

First Citizen. Yes, a knife, but not for the pitiable whore! What has she done? Nothing! It's her empty belly makes her whore and beg. A knife for the men who buy the flesh of our wives and daughters! Woe to them who lust after the daughters of citizens! You have rumblings in your bellies, they have stomach cramps; you have holes in your jackets, they have warm coats; you have calluses on your hands, they have silk gloves. Ergo: you work and they sit on their asses; ergo: you earn the bread and they steal it; ergo: when you want back a few coins of your property they've stolen you have to go whoring and begging; ergo: they are thieves and must be killed!

Third Citizen. The only blood in their veins is what they've sucked from us. Once they told us: "Kill the aristocrats, they're the preying wolves!" We killed the aristocrats and hung them from street lamps. They told us: "The Girondins are starving you out!" We guillotined the Girondins. But they're the ones who stripped the bodies naked, and here we stand bare and freezing as ever. We'll peel the skin from their thighs and make pants for ourselves. We'll burn the fat from their asses to make us richer soups. Away! Kill a man without a hole in his jacket!

First Citizen. Kill a man who reads and writes!

Second Citizen. Kill a man who walks like an aristocrat!

All [*screaming*]. Kill! Kill!

A YOUNG MAN *is dragged past.*

Several Voices. He's got a handkerchief! An aristocrat! To the street lamp with him! To the street lamp!

Second Citizen. What's this? He doesn't blow his nose through his fingers? To the street lamp with him!

Young Man. Gentlemen! Gentlemen!

Second Citizen. There are no gentlemen here! To the street lamp with him!

Several Voices [*sing*].

> Those who lie below the ground,
> They will soon by worms be found;
> Better by the neck to wave
> Than rot below in a dismal grave!

Young Man. Mercy!

Third Citizen. It's only a game with a hemp noose around your neck! It only takes a minute; we're more merciful than you aristocrats. We spend our lives at the end of a rope, hang there for sixty years, kicking—but we'll cut ourselves free. To the street lamp with him!

Young Man. Hanging me on a light won't make things any brighter for you.

Citizens. Bravo! Well said!

Several Voices. Let him go!

THE YOUNG MAN *runs off.* ROBESPIERRE *enters accompanied by* WOMEN *and* SANS-CULOTTES.

Robespierre. What is it, citizens?

Third Citizen. What is it you'll give us, you mean? Those few drops of blood shed in August and September still haven't turned the people's cheeks red. The guillotine is too slow. We need a hailstorm.

First Citizen. Our wives and children cry out for bread, we want to feed them on the flesh of the aristocrats. Kill every man without a hole in his jacket!

All. Kill! Kill!

Robespierre. In the name of the law!

First Citizen. What is the law?

Robespierre. The will of the people.

First Citizen. We are the people and we don't want the law; ergo: our will is the law; ergo: in the name of the law there is no more law; ergo: kill!

Several Voices. Listen to Aristides there! Listen to the incorruptible Robespierre!

A Woman. Listen to the Messiah who is sent to choose

and judge; he will strike the wicked with the sharp of his sword. His eyes are the eyes of truth, his hands the hands of justice!

Robespierre. Poor, virtuous people! You do your duty. You sacrifice your enemies. People—how great a people you are! You reveal yourselves amidst lightning and thunderclaps. But, my people, your blows must not wound your own bodies; in your rage you must not murder yourselves. You can be overcome only by your own strength, and your enemies know that. Your legislators watch you, they will guide your hands; their eyes cannot be deceived, your hands cannot fail. Come with me to the Jacobin Club! They, your brothers, will extend their arms to greet you, and we shall hold bloody judgment over our enemies.

Many Voices. To the Jacobin Club! Long live Robespierre!

All go off.

Simon. Alone—all, all alone! [*He tries to rise.*]

Wife. There. [*She supports him.*]

Simon. Ah, my gentle Baucis! Why must you pour coals of fire upon my head?

Wife. Stand up now!

Simon. Why do you turn away? Can you forgive me, my Portia? Did I strike you? It was not my hand nor arm but my madness did it.

His madness is poor Hamlet's enemy.

Then Hamlet did it not; Hamlet denies it. Where is our daughter, where is our little girl?

Wife. There, around the corner.

Simon. Let us get her then. Come, my virtuous wife.

They both go off.

SCENE III—*The Jacobin Club*

DEPUTY FROM LYONS. Our brothers from Lyons have sent us here to pour our bitter indignance in your ears. We do not know whether the cart which drove Ronsin to the guillotine was the hearse of Liberty, but we do know that since that day the murderers of Chalier have walked the streets as safely as if no grave awaited them. Have you forgotten that Lyons is a stain upon the soil of France which must be covered over with the limbs of traitors? Have you forgotten that this whore of kings can only wash her scabs in the waters of the Rhône? Have you forgotten that this flood of Revolution must cause Pitt's navies in the Mediterranean to run aground on the bodies of aristocrats? You are murdering the Revolution with your compassion. The breath of an aristocrat is the death-rattle of Freedom. A coward dies for the Republic, a Jacobin kills for it. I tell you this: that unless we find in you the driving power of the tenth of August, of September, and the thirty-first of May, there remains for us, as for the patriot Galliard, only the suicidal dagger of Cato.

Applause and confused cries.

A *Jacobin.* We will drink the cup of Socrates with you!

Legendre [*springs to the tribune*]. We have no need to look to Lyons for traitors. These people who wear silken clothes, who ride about in carriages, who sit in loges in the theatre and speak according to the Dictionary of the Academy, have for several days now felt their heads secure upon their shoulders. They are witty and say that Marat and Chalier must be helped to a second martyrdom, that they must be guillotined in effigy.

There is a violent commotion in the assembly.

Several Voices. Those men are dead—their tongues have guillotined them.

Legendre. May the blood of these saints be upon them! I now ask the present members of the Committee of Public Safety: Since when have your ears grown so deaf——

Collot d'Herbois [*interrupts him*]. And I ask *you*, Legendre: Whose voice gives breath to such thoughts that they may come alive and speak such treason? It is time we tore off our masks! Listen! The cause accuses its effect, the voice its own echo, and the premise its conclusion. The Committee of Public Safety understands more logic than that, Legendre. Calm yourself! The busts of these saints will remain where they are, they shall transform traitors into stone like Medusa heads.

Robespierre. I demand the tribune.

The Jacobins. Listen! Listen to the incorruptible Robespierre!

Robespierre. We have waited only for the cry of indignation to resound from all sides before we spoke. Our eyes were open, we saw the enemy arm himself and rise up, but we did not sound the alarm; we allowed the people to watch over itself; it has not slept, it has taken up arms and made clamor. We allowed the enemy to come forth from his ambush, we allowed him to draw near; he stands there now, open and unconcealed in the bright light of day; every stroke will strike home, he is dead the moment you see him.—I have told you all this before: the internal enemies of the Republic have fallen into two factions, as if into two armies. Under banners of different colors and by different ways they march toward the same end. One of these factions no longer exists. In their affected madness they sought to cast aside as worn-out weaklings the most proven Patriots of the Republic in order to rob us of our strongest allies. They declared war on the Godhead and on property to create a diversion in favor of the kings. They parodied the sublime drama of the Revolution to discredit it with calculated excesses. Hébert's triumph would have brought chaos on the Republic, and despotism would have been satisfied. The sword of the law has struck down that traitor. But what do those foreign enemies of the Republic care as long as they still have criminals of another sort to achieve the same end? We have done nothing so long as there is another faction still to be annihilated. This faction is the opposite of the other. They would drive us to be weak; their battle cry is: "Mercy." They would tear from the people their arms and the strength they need to wield those arms, and deliver them up to the kings naked and unnerved. The arm of the Republic is Terror, the strength of the Republic is Virtue—Virtue because without it Terror is pernicious; Terror because without it Virtue is powerless. Terror is the consequence of Virtue, it is nothing other than swift, stern, and unswerving justice. They say that Terror is the weapon of despotism and that therefore our government is a despotism. Yes! But only in so far as the swords in the hands of heroes who fight for Freedom are like unto the sabers with which the satellites of tyrants are armed. If the despot rules his brutelike subjects by means of Terror, then, as a despot, he is justified. If by means of the same Terror you destroy the enemies of Freedom, then you, as founders of the Republic, are no less justified. The government of this Revolution is the despotism of Freedom against tyranny. Certain persons call out for mercy toward the Royalists! Mercy for villains? No! Mercy for the innocent, mercy for the weak, mercy for the unfortunate, mercy for mankind! Only peaceable citizens deserve protection from society. Only Republicans are citizens in a Republic, Royalists and foreigners are enemies. To punish the oppressors of mankind is mercy; to forgive them, barbarism. Every sign of false sensitivity appears to me to be sighs that wing their way to England or to Austria. But not content to disarm the people's hands, they also seek to poison the purest sources of our strength through vice. This is the subtlest, the most dangerous, and the most abominable attack of all upon Freedom. Vice is the aristocracy's mark of Cain. In a Republic this becomes not merely a moral but a political crime as well; the man of vice is a political enemy of Freedom, he is all the more dangerous the greater the services he appears to perform. The most dangerous citizen is the one who finds it easier to wear out a dozen red caps than do a single good deed. You will understand me more easily if you recall those persons who once lived in attics but now drive about in carriages and fornicate with former marquises and baronesses. We may well ask whether the people have been plundered, or whether the golden hands of kings have been pressed when we see the legislators of the people parade about with all the vices and all the luxuries of former courtiers, when we see all these marquises and counts of the Revolution marrying rich wives, giving sumptuous banquets, gambling, keeping servants, and wearing priceless clothes. We may well be amazed when we hear of their empty exhibits of wit, their esthetic pretensions, and their good manners. A short time ago one of them parodied Tacitus in a most shameless way;

I could answer out of Sallust and travesty Catiline, though I think there are no more strokes necessary: the portrait is complete. We will have no compromise, no armistice with men whose only thought was to plunder the people, and who hoped to carry out this plan of plunder with impunity, men for whom the Republic was a speculation and the Revolution a trade! Terrified by the torrent of examples we have made, they seek softly now to mitigate the hand of our justice. We are to believe that each says to himself: "We are not virtuous enough to be so terrible. O lawgiving philosophers, have mercy on our weaknesses! I dare not say to you that I am vicious; rather I say to you: 'Be not so inhuman!' "—Calm yourselves, my virtue-loving people, O Patriots, be calm! Say to your brethren in Lyons: "The sword of the law will not rust in the hands of him to whom it was entrusted!" We shall set our Republic a great example.

General applause.

Many Voices. Long live the Republic! Long live Robespierre!

President. The session is closed.

SCENE IV—A *street*

LACROIX. LEGENDRE

LACROIX. What have you done, Legendre! Do you realize whose heads you've thrown down with those busts of yours?

Legendre. A few dandies and some elegant women, that's all.

Lacroix. You're a suicide, a shadow that kills its original with itself.

Legendre. I don't understand.

Lacroix. I thought Collot spoke plainly enough.

Legendre. What does that matter? He was drunk again.

Lacroix. Fools, children, and—well?—drunk men tell the truth. Whom do you think Robespierre meant when he spoke of Catiline?

Legendre. Well?

Lacroix. It's simple enough. The atheists and extremists have been sent to the guillotine; but the people have not been helped, they run about in the streets barefoot and swear they'll make shoes out of the aristocrats' skins. The thermometer of the guillotine must not fall; a few degrees lower and the Committee of Public Safety can make its bed on the Place de la Révolution.

Legendre. What have my busts to do with all this?

Lacroix. You still don't see? You've made the counter-revolution officially known, you've forced the Committee to action, you've led their hands. The people are a Minotaur that must be fed with corpses weekly or they will eat the Committee alive.

Legendre. Where is Danton?

Lacroix. How should I know? He's looking for the Venus de' Medici piecemeal among all the whores of the Palais Royal; he's making a mosaic, as he puts it. God only knows what limb he's working at now. Pity that nature cuts up beauty in such small pieces, like Medea her brothers, and deposits them haphazardly in people's bodies.—Let's go to the Palais Royal!

SCENE V—*A room*

DANTON. MARION

MARION. No, leave me alone. I'll sit here at your feet. I'll tell you a story.

Danton. You might put your lips to better use.

Marion. No, leave me here like this.—My mother was a clever woman; she always told me that purity was the loveliest of virtues. When people would come to our house and begin talking about certain things, she always sent me out of the room; and when I asked her what they meant, she said I should be ashamed asking such questions; then when she gave me books to read I almost always had to leave out certain pages. But I could read as much of the Bible as I wanted because everything there was holy. Still there were parts of it that I never understood. I didn't want to ask anybody, so I brooded over them myself. Then the spring came; there was something

happening all around me in which I had no share. I was
in an atmosphere all my own, and it almost stifled me.
I looked at my body; at times it seemed that there were
two of me, and then they would melt again into one.
About this time a young man came to the house. He was
very beautiful and often talked to me about silly things.
I didn't know exactly what they meant, but I had to
laugh. My mother made him come often, and that pleased
us both. Finally we didn't see why we shouldn't as soon lie
next to one another between two sheets as sit beside one
another on two chairs. I enjoyed that much more than
his conversation and couldn't understand why they wanted
me to be content with the smaller pleasures rather than
the larger one. We did it secretly. And so it went on. But
I became like a sea that swallows down everything and
sinks deeper and deeper into itself. The only fact that
existed for me was my opposite, all men melted into one
body. It was my nature, what choice did I have? Finally
he noticed. He came one morning and kissed me as though
he wanted to suffocate me; his arms wound around my
neck, I was terribly afraid. Then he let go of me and
laughed and said that he had almost done a foolish thing;
that I should keep my dress and wear it, that it would
wear out soon enough by itself, and that he didn't want
to spoil my fun for me too soon, because it was all I had.
Then he went away; again I didn't know what he meant.
That evening I sat at the window; I'm very sensitive, and
the only hold I have on my surroundings is through what
I feel; I sank into the waves of the sunset. A crowd of
people came down the street then, children running ahead
of them and women looking out of their windows. I looked
down: they were carrying him past in a basket, the moon
was reflected on his pale forehead, his hair was wet—
he had drowned himself. All I could do was cry.—It was
the only time that my life ever stopped. Other people
have Sundays and weekdays, they work six days and pray
on the seventh; once every year on their birthdays they
become sentimental and every year they think about the
New Year. I don't understand that at all: I know nothing
of such breaks in time, of change. I am always only one
thing, an unbroken longing and grasping, a flame, a

stream. My mother died of grief. People were always pointing at me because of it. That's stupid. There's only one thing that matters, whether it's our bodies, or holy pictures, or flowers, or children's toys. It's all the same feeling: the person who enjoys the most, prays the most.

Danton. Why can't I contain every part of your beauty inside me, hold it in my arms?

Marion. Danton, your lips have eyes.

Danton. I wish I were a part of air that I could bathe you all about in my flood, break myself on every cape of your exquisite body.

LACROIX, ADELAIDE, *and* ROSALIE *enter.*

Lacroix [*remains in the doorway*]. You will excuse me for laughing, but I can't help myself.

Danton [*angrily*]. Well?

Lacroix. I was just thinking of the street.

Danton. So?

Lacroix. Well, there were two dogs in the street just now, a great Dane and an Italian lapdog; they were having a go at it.

Danton. What do you mean by that?

Lacroix. It merely occurred to me and I couldn't help laughing. It was quite edifying! Girls were looking out of their windows—one should be careful and never even let them sit in the sun: flies are liable to do it in their hands; it might give them cause for thought.—Legendre and I have gone through almost every cell here. The little Nuns of the Revelation through the Flesh clung to our coat-tails and asked our blessing. Legendre is giving one of them her penance now, though he may have to fast for a month afterwards himself. I've brought two of our priestesses of the body along with me.

Marion. Good day, Mlle. Adelaide! Good day, Mlle. Rosalie!

Rosalie. It's been a long time since we had the pleasure.

Marion. Yes, I'm sorry too.

Adelaide. My God, we never have a minute free.

Danton [*to* ROSALIE]. Well, your hips seem to get better by the day, my dear.

Rosalie. One improves with practice.

Lacroix. What's the difference between the ancient and the modern Adonis?

Danton. And Adelaide has become very virtuously interesting; a charming change. Her face resembles a fig leaf that she holds up to cover her entire body. A fig tree like that throws a most wonderful shade on so busy a thoroughfare.

Adelaide. I'd be nothing but a country road if not for monsieur who——

Danton. I understand; just don't be a bitch, my sweet!

Lacroix. No, listen! A modern Adonis isn't torn by a boar, he's torn by sows; his wound isn't received in the thigh any more but in the groin; and instead of roses, buds of mercury sprout from his blood.

Danton. And Mlle. Rosalie is a restored torso, of which only the hips and feet are genuine antique. She's a magnetic needle: what the pole of the head repels, the pole of the feet attracts; her middle is an equator, where everyone who crosses the line must baptize his parts in mercuric chloride.

Lacroix. Two sisters of mercy—each serving in her own hospital, that is to say in their own bodies.

Rosalie. Shame on you, making our ears turn red!

Adelaide. You ought to have more manners!

ADELAIDE *and* ROSALIE *go off.*

Danton. Good night, you pretty children!

Lacroix. Good night, you mines of mercury!

Danton. I feel sorry for them, they came for their supper.

Lacroix. Listen, Danton, I've just come from the Jacobin Club.

Danton. Is that all?

Lacroix. The delegates from Lyons read a proclamation; they said the only thing left them to do is wrap themselves in their togas like Caesar; each of them making a face as though to say to his neighbor: "The knife won't hurt, Paetus!" Legendre cried out that they wanted to break the busts of Chalier and Marat. I think he wants to paint his face red again; he got through the Terror unharmed, and children tug at his coattails in the streets.

Danton. And Robespierre?

Lacroix. He drummed his fingers on the tribune and said that Virtue must rule through Terror. The phrase made my neck feel raw.

Danton. It planes boards for the guillotine.

Lacroix. And Collot cried out like a man possessed that they must tear off their masks.

Danton. I'm afraid their faces would come with them.

PARIS *enters.*

Lacroix. What is it, Fabricus?

Paris. I went straight from the Jacobin Club to Robespierre and demanded an explanation. He tried to look like Brutus sacrificing his sons. He spoke in general terms about duty, and said that where Freedom is concerned he has no personal considerations and would sacrifice everything, himself, his sons, his brothers, his friends.

Danton. That's obvious enough; one has only to reverse the order, putting him at the bottom holding the ladder for his friends. We owe Legendre our thanks for having got it out of him.

Lacroix. The Hébertists aren't dead yet and the people are still starving; that's a dreadful lever. The scale of blood must not be allowed to grow lighter unless we want to see the Committee of Public Safety hanged from it; it has need of ballast, it needs a heavy head.

Danton. I know, I know—the Revolution is like Saturn, it devours its own children. [*After a moment of thought*] And yet, I don't think they would dare.

Lacroix. Danton, you're a dead saint. But the Revolution doesn't recognize relics. It's tossed the bones of kings into the streets, broken statues in churches—do you think they'll let you stand here a monument?

Danton. My name! The people!

Lacroix. Your name! You're a moderate, so am I, and Camille and Philippeau and Hérault. Moderation to these people is the same as weakness; they kill all stragglers. The tailors from the Section of Red Caps would feel all Roman history in their needles if the Man of September were a moderate in regard to them.

Danton. Very true, and besides that—the people are like a child: they have to break everything open to see what's inside it.

Lacroix. And then, too, Danton, we're vicious people, according to Robespierre, that is, we enjoy ourselves; but the people are virtuous, that is, they *don't* enjoy themselves, because work dulls their organs of pleasure; they don't get drunk because they haven't the money, and they don't go whoring because they stink of cheese and herring and the girls don't like that.

Danton. They hate people who enjoy themselves just as eunuchs hate men.

Lacroix. They call us thieves, and [*Bending toward* DANTON's *ear.*], just between us, there may be something to that. Robespierre and the people will be virtuous. Saint-Just will write a novel—that is, deliver one of his interminable reports—and Barère will deliver his usual speech which will send someone to the guillotine and so drape the Convention in a mantle of blood—I can see it all.

Danton. You're dreaming. They've never had courage *without* me, so how can they have any *against* me? The Revolution isn't over yet, they might still need me; they'll hang me in the Arsenal for future reference.

Lacroix. We must do something.

Danton. We'll see.

Lacroix. We'll see when we're lost.

Marion [*to* DANTON]. Your lips have grown cold: your words have stifled your kisses.

Danton [*to* MARION]. My God, the time we've lost! But it was worth every minute! [*To* LACROIX.] I'll see Robespierre; I'll make him angry, he can't keep his mouth shut then. Tomorrow, then! Good night, my friends! Good night! I thank you!

Lacroix. Hurry, my friends, hurry! Good night, Danton! A woman's thighs will be your guillotine, and her mound of Venus your Tarpeian rock.   [*He goes off with* PARIS.

SCENE VI—A *room*

ROBESPIERRE. DANTON. PARIS

ROBESPIERRE. I tell you that anyone who tries to hinder me when my sword is drawn is my enemy—no matter what his intentions. Any man who keeps me from defending myself is my murderer just as surely as if he attacked me.

Danton. Where self-defense ends murder begins. I see no reason why we should go on killing.

Robespierre. The social Revolution is not yet complete; you dig your own grave, leaving a Revolution half-finished. The aristocrats are still alive, the healthy strength of the people must replace this degenerate, pleasure-loving class. Vice must be punished and Virtue must rule through Terror.

Danton. I don't understand your word "punishment." You and your Virtue, Robespierre! You've never taken money, you've never incurred any debts, you've never slept with a woman, you've always worn a decent coat and never got yourself drunk. Robespierre, you are disgustingly virtuous. I'd be ashamed to walk around between heaven and earth for thirty years with that moral expression on my face, and only for the miserable pleasure of finding others worse than myself. Isn't there something inside you that whispers sometimes, quietly, secretly, that you lie, Robespierre, you lie?

Robespierre. My conscience is clean.

Danton. Conscience is a mirror that monkeys torment themselves in front of. We all get ourselves up as best we can, and then go out and find fun in our own way. It's worth the trouble, believe me! We all have the right to protect ourselves when someone comes along to spoil our fun. What makes you think you have the right to turn the guillotine into a washtub for other people's dirty linens and scrub spots from their clothes with their cut-off heads? And just because you've always worn a well-brushed coat? Yes, you can always defend yourself when they spit on it or tear holes in it; but what right have you when they leave you in peace? If they're not ashamed to go around as they do, does that give you the right to send them to their graves? Are you God's Special Deputy? And if you can't bear up under the sight like your Good Lord God, then cover your eyes with your handkerchief.

Robespierre. Are you denying Virtue?

Danton. Yes, and vice, too. All men are epicureans, either crude or refined, as the case may be: Christ was the most refined of them all. That is the only difference that I can discern between men. Every man acts according to his own nature, that is, he does what does him good. It's cruel, isn't it, my incorruptible friend, to take you down like this.

Robespierre. Danton, there are certain times when vice becomes high treason.

Danton. But for God's sake, you mustn't condemn it, that would be ungrateful; you owe it far too much, by contrast, I mean. Furthermore, according to your own notions, even *our* deeds must be of use to the Republic, since one mustn't strike both guilty and innocent alike.

Robespierre. Whoever said an innocent man had been condemned?

Danton. Did you hear that, Fabricus? No innocent man condemned! [*He leaves; to* PARIS *while going.*] We haven't a minute to lose; we must declare ourselves!

DANTON *and* PARIS *go off.*

Robespierre [*alone*]. Go on! He thinks he can halt the horses of the Revolution outside a brothel, like a coachman with his jaded nags; but they'll have enough strength to drag him to the guillotine.—To take me down, he said! According to my own notions!—But wait! Wait! Is it really that?—They'll say that his gigantic figure cast too great a shadow across me, and for that reason I had to order him from the sun.—And what if they were right? Is it so necessary? Yes, yes! The Republic! He must be got out of the light.—It's laughable how each thought of mine suspects the other.—He must be got out of the light. A man who stands still in a crowd pressing forward is as much an obstacle as if he opposed it: that man will be trampled under foot. We will not permit the Ship of

Revolution to founder on the shallow notions and mud-
banks of these people; the hand must be hacked away that
would hold it back—and if he grasps at it with his
teeth . . . Down with the class that has stolen the
clothes of the dead aristocracy and inherited their sores!—
No Virtue! Take me down! My own notions!—It keeps
coming back to me. Why can't I rid myself of these
thoughts? He points his bloody finger at me here, here!
I can wrap it in as many bandages as I like, but the blood
will always come through. [*After a pause.*] I don't know
which part of me is lying to the other. [*He goes to the
window.*] Night snores over the earth and tosses itself
about in dreamful dreams. Thoughts, desires, scarcely
imagined, confused and formless, that crept timidly from
the light of day, take shape now and steal into the silent
house of dreams. They push open the doors, they look out
of the windows, they become half flesh and blood, their
limbs stretch in sleep, their lips murmur.—And is our
waking anything but a dream, a clear dream? Are we not
all sleepwalkers? What are our actions but the actions of
a dream, only more clear, more definite, more complete?
Who will blame us for that? The mind in a single hour
accomplishes more deeds of thought than the sluggish
organism of our body can imitate in a year. Sin is in our
thoughts. Whether the thought will grow into deed, or
the body imitate it—is a matter of chance.

SAINT-JUST *enters.*

Robespierre. Who's there, in the dark? Ho! A light!
Saint-Just. Do you know me by my voice?
Robespierre. Oh, it's you, Saint-Just!

A SERVANT GIRL *brings in a light.*

Saint-Just. Were you alone?
Robespierre. Danton just now left.
Saint-Just. I met him on the way in the Palais Royal.
He was trying out his Revolution face and talking in
epigrams; fraternizing with the sans-culottes, whores running along behind his legs, and the people standing about
whispering in one another's ears what he'd said.—We're
going to lose the advantage of the initial attack. How

much longer do you want to delay? We'll act without you. We've made our decision.

Robespierre. What do you plan to do?

Saint-Just. We will summon the Legislative Committee, the Committee of General Security, and the Committee of Public Safety to a special session.

Robespierre. All this fuss!

Saint-Just. We must bury the distinguished corpse with dignity, like priests, not like murderers; nor may we mutilate it in any way, it must be buried entire.

Robespierre. You will speak more clearly!

Saint-Just. We must inter him in full armor, and slaughter his horses and slaves on the burial mound: Lacroix——

Robespierre. An absolute scoundrel, former barrister's clerk, and now Lieutenant-General of France. Continue!

Saint-Just. Hérault-Séchelles.

Robespierre. A handsome head!

Saint-Just. The handsomely painted capital at the head of the Constitution; we have no further need of such ornaments; he will be obliterated. Philippeau.—Camille.

Robespierre. Camille, too?

Saint-Just [*hands him a paper*]. That was my reaction at first, too. Read this!

Robespierre. Le vieux Cordelier. Is that all? He's a child; he laughed at you.

Saint-Just. Read this, here! [*He shows him the place.*]

Robespierre [*reading*]. "This bloody Messiah Robespierre on his calvary between the two thieves Couthon and Collot—where he sacrifices but will not himself be sacrificed. The prayerful sisters of the guillotine stand at his feet like Mary and the Magdalene. Saint-Just, like John the Beloved, embraces his neck and makes known to the Convention the apocalyptic revelations of his master; he bears his head as though it contained the Sacred Host."

Saint-Just. I'll make him carry it like Saint-Denis.

Robespierre [*continues reading*]. "Are we to believe that the immaculate frockcoat of the Messiah is the winding sheet of France, and that his fingers twitching on the tribune are the knives of the guillotine?—And you, Barère, who once said that coins would be minted on the

Place de la Révolution! But let's not dig up that old sack
again. He's a widow with already half a dozen husbands,
all of whom he has helped bury. But what can we do?
It's a gift of his: like Hippocrates he can see the livid
aspects of death in a man's face six months in advance.
And who would want to sit with corpses and smell their
putrefying odors?"—And so, you, too, Camille?—Away with
them! Quick! Only the dead cannot return.—Have you
prepared the indictment?

Saint-Just. That's easy enough. You gave full indication
of it at the Jacobin Club.

Robespierre. I wanted to frighten them.

Saint-Just. I need only carry out your threats; the
forgers will stuff them on hors d'œuvres and the foreigners
on dessert.—The meal will kill them, I can assure you.

Robespierre. Quickly then, tomorrow! No long death
agonies! I've grown sensitive these last few days.—Only
be quick about it!

SAINT-JUST *goes out.*

Robespierre [alone]. Yes, the bloody Messiah who sacrifices himself but will not himself be sacrificed.—*He* re-
deemed them with *His* blood, and I will redeem them with
their own. He created them sinners, and I take the sin
on myself. He suffered the ecstasy of pain, and I the torment of the executioner. Who denied himself, He or I?—
And yet there's something foolish in the thought.—Why
do we always look to *Him* as an example? Truly the Son
of Man is crucified in us all; we all wrestle in bloody
agony in our own Gardens of Gethsemane; but not one
of us redeems the other with his wounds.—O Camille!—
They are all leaving me—the world is empty and void—
I am alone.

ACT TWO

SCENE I—A *room*

DANTON, LACROIX, PHILIPPEAU, PARIS, CAMILLE DESMOULINS

CAMILLE. Hurry, Danton, we have no time to lose!

Danton [*dressing himself*]. And yet, time loses us!—How tedious it is always to have to put one's shirt on first and then pull up one's trousers; to spend the night in bed and then in the morning have to crawl out again and always place one foot in front of the other—and no one even imagines it could be otherwise. It's very sad; millions have already done so and millions more are destined to do so; and besides that we consist of two halves, each doing the same thing, so everything happens twice—it's very sad.

Camille. You're talking like a child.

Danton. The dying often become childish.

Lacroix. This delay of yours is plunging you into ruin, and you're dragging your friends with you. Tell the cowards the time has come to rally round you, call them from the plains as well as from the mountains! Shout against the tyranny of the Committee, talk of daggers, invoke Brutus, that way you'll rouse the Tribunes and even rally round you those who were threatened as accomplices of Hébert! You must give in to your anger. At least don't let us die disarmed and humiliated like that disgraceful Hébert!

Danton. You have a bad memory, you called me a dead saint. You were more justified than you realize. I've been to see the Section leaders; they were respectful, but more like undertakers. I'm a relic, and relics are tossed into the streets—you were right.

Lacroix. Why have you let it come to this?

Danton. To this? Yes, of course; it finally began to bore me. Always to go about in the same coat and make the same kind of face! It's pitiable. To be a miserable instrument on which each string gives out only a single note!—I couldn't stand it any longer. I wanted to make myself

comfortable. And I've succeeded; the Revolution is retir-
ing me, but not in the way I had expected.—Besides, on
what can we support ourselves? Our whores might still
find a place with the prayerful sisters of the guillotine;
otherwise I can think of nothing else. You can figure it all
out on your fingers: the Jacobins have declared Virtue the
order of the day; the Cordeliers call me Hébert's executioner; the Commune does penance; the Committee—
that might have been a way!—but there was the thirty-
first of May; they wouldn't soften willingly. Robespierre
is the dogma of the Revolution that can't be stricken.
But that wouldn't work either. We didn't make the Revolution, the Revolution made us.—And even if it could
work—I'd rather suffer the guillotine myself than make
others suffer it. I'm disgusted with it all; why must men
fight one another? We should sit down and be at peace
together. I think there was a mistake in the creation of
us; there's something missing in us that I haven't a name
for—but we'll never find it by burrowing in one another's
entrails, so why break open our bodies? We're a miserable
lot of alchemists!

Camille. More pathetically put, you would have said:
"How long must Mankind in its eternal starvation devour
its own flesh?" Or: "How long must we who are shipwrecked suck the blood from one another's veins in our
unquenchable thirst?" Or: "How long must we algebraists
of the flesh in our search for the unknown and eternally
withheld x write our accounts with mangled limbs?"

Danton. You are a powerful echo.

Camille. It's true, a pistol shot does make as much
noise as a clap of thunder. All the better for you then that
I stay with you.

Philippeau. And France stay with her executioners?

Danton. Do you think it really matters? They're well off
enough even so. Yes, they're unhappy; but what more can
one ask to make himself compassionate, noble, virtuous
or witty, or in general simply not bored with it all?—What
does it matter whether they die on the guillotine or of
fever or of old age! But there's still something to be said
for leaving the stage with a good spring in your step and
a fine gesture and hearing the applause of the spectators be-

hind you. It's an agreeable way to go and it also suits us: we stand on the stage all our lives, even though in the end we are finally stabbed in earnest.—It's not so terrible to have our life's span cut down a bit; especially since the coat was too long, and our limbs never quite filled it out. Life becomes an epigram; that makes it bearable. Who has either breath or imagination for an epic in fifty or sixty cantos? It's time we started drinking our little bottle of elixir out of liqueur glasses instead of tubs; that way at least we'd get a mouthful, rather than have the few drops lost in the bottom of the clumsy vessel.—Finally—my God, I can't hold it in any longer!—finally it isn't worth the trouble, life isn't worth the effort it costs us to keep it going.

Paris. Escape, then, Danton!

Danton. If I could take my country with me on the soles of my shoes, yes.—But finally—and this is the main point—they wouldn't dare lay hand on me. Good-bye! Good-bye!

DANTON *and* CAMILLE *go off.*

Philippeau. There he goes.

Lacroix. And doesn't believe a word of what he said. He's lazy! He'd rather be sent to the guillotine than . . . make a speech.

Paris. What can we do?

Lacroix. Go home and like Lucretia study to make an honorable end.

SCENE II—A *promenade*

A CITIZEN. Did you know that my virtuous Jacqueline— I mean, Corn—— what I meant was, Cor——.

Simon. Cornelia, Citizen, Cornelia.

Citizen. My virtuous Cornelia has blessed me with a son.

Simon. Blessed the Republic with a son.

Citizen. The Republic? No, no, that's too general; one might almost say——

Simon. That's the point, the particular must contribute to the general. . . .

Citizen. Yes, yes, that's what my wife says too.

Ballad-Singer [*sings*].

    Tell me then, tell me then,

    What is it now that pleases men?

Citizen. Now it's the name for the boy, we can't agree.

Simon. Why not call him Pike Marat?

Ballad-Singer [*sings*].

    Bent with sorrow, bent with care,

    To sweat all day in foul despair,

    Till the evening comes again.

Citizen. I'd really like three—there's something about the number three—now let me see, I'd like a name that's useful and one that's honest; I know: Plough, and Robespierre. But now the third . . .

Simon. Pike.

Citizen. Many thanks, neighbor! Pike, Plough, Robespierre—fine names; sounds good.

Simon. I tell you, the breasts of your Cornelia will, like the udders of the Roman she-wolf—no, that won't do: Romulus was a tyrant, so that won't do.

They walk on.

A Beggar [*sings*].

    A handful of earth and a little piece of moss . . .

Kind gentlemen, lovely ladies!

First Gentleman. Why don't you work, you lazy lout? You look well enough fed!

Second Gentleman. Here! [*Gives him some money.*] Why, his hands are soft as velvet! The shameless thief!

Beggar. Sir, where did you get your coat from?

Second Gentleman. Work, my good fellow, work! You could have one, too; I'll give you some work if you like. Come to me at——

Beggar. And, sir, why did you work?

Second Gentleman. You fool, to have the coat, of course!

Beggar. You tortured yourself for a luxury; because a coat like that is a luxury when a rag would do just as well.

Second Gentleman. Of course, otherwise you'd never get on.

Beggar. I'd never be such a fool! The work I'd have to

do wouldn't make it worth it. The sun there on the
corner's nice and warm, and it's free. [*Sings.*]

    A handful of earth and a little piece of moss . . .

    Rosalie [*to* ADELAIDE]. Hurry up, here come some
soldiers! We've had nothing warm in our bellies since
yesterday.

    Beggar [*sings*].

        Is all that is left of my profit and my loss!
Kind gentlemen, lovely ladies!

    Soldier. Halt! Where're you girls off to? [*To* ROSALIE.]
How old are you?

    Rosalie. Old as my little finger.

    Soldier. Sharp, aren't you!

    Rosalie. And aren't you blunt!

    Soldier. What do you say I use you for a whetstone
then? [*Sings.*]

        Christina, O Christina mine,
        Does the pain hurt you sore, hurt you sore?
        Does the pain hurt you sore?

    Rosalie [*sings*].

        For shame not, my sweet soldier dear,
        I wish that I could have more, have more!
        I wish that I could have more!

    DANTON *and* CAMILLE *enter.*

    Danton. How happy they look!—I smell something
here in the air; like the sun hatching out lechery.—It
makes a man want to get down there, doesn't it? Rip off
his pants and go at it like dogs in the street!

    They go on.

    Young Gentleman. Ah, madame, the sound of a bell,
the light of evening on the trees, the twinkle of the first
star . . .

    Madame. The fragrance of a flower! These natural
pleasures, this pure enjoyment of nature! [*To her daughter*
EUGÉNIE.] You see, Eugénie, only Virtue has eyes for such
things.

    Eugénie [*kisses her mother's hand*]. Oh, Mama, I see
only you.

    Madame. That's a good child.

Young Gentleman [*whispers in* EUGÉNIE's *ear*]. Do you see the pretty lady over there with the old gentleman?

Eugénie. I know her.

Young Gentleman. They say the hairdresser did her hair *à l'enfant.*

Eugénie [*laughs*]. Naughty gossip!

Young Gentleman. And the old gentleman walks along beside her; he sees the bud swelling and takes it out in the sun for a walk, thinking he was the thundershower that made it grow.

Eugénie. How indelicate of you! I feel I should blush.

Young Gentleman. That could make me grow pale.

They go off.

Danton [*to* CAMILLE]. Don't expect anything serious out of me! I don't understand why people don't just plant themselves in the street and laugh in one another's faces. I should think they would have to be laughing from their windows and from their graves, and that heaven itself would burst, and the earth roll over in laughter.

They go off.

First Gentleman. I assure you it is a most extraordinary discovery! It gives the technical arts an entirely new aspect. Mankind hurries with giant strides toward his higher destiny.

Second Gentleman. Have you seen the new play? There's a Babylonian tower, a great confusion of arches and steps and passages—and they blow it all up into the air just as easily and cleverly as you could imagine. You grow dizzy at every step. What an extraordinary brain that invented it! [*He stands there, suddenly perplexed.*]

First Gentleman. Why, what's the matter with you?

Second Gentleman. Oh, nothing, nothing at all! Would you reach me your hand, sir! The puddles in the street, you know. There! Thank you, sir! I almost didn't get across them! It could have been dangerous!

First Gentleman. Surely you weren't afraid?

Second Gentleman. Well, you see, sir, the earth has nothing but a thin crust—a thin, thin crust. I always fancy I might fall through a hole like that if I were to

step into it.—One must be careful where one steps. One
might break through! But you *must* go to see the play;
I highly recommend it!

SCENE III—A *room*

DANTON. CAMILLE. LUCILLE

CAMILLE. I tell you that unless they have wooden copies
of everything, scattered about in theatres, concert halls,
and art exhibits, people have neither eyes nor ears for it.
Let someone carve out a marionette so that they can see
the strings that pull it up and down and with each awk-
ward movement from its joints hear it roar out an iambic
line; what a character, they'll cry out, what consistency!
Take a minor sentiment, a maxim, a notion, and dress it
up in coat and trousers, make pairs of hands and feet for
it, color its face and permit the thing to moan and agonize
about for three whole acts until at last it has either
married or shot itself dead—and they will cry out that
it was ideal! Fiddle them out an opera which reproduces
the rising and sinking of the human soul as a clay pipe
with water reproduces the sounds of the nightingale—oh,
what art, they will cry out!—Take these same people from
the theatre and put them on the street and they'll grow
pained with pitiful reality!—They forget their Lord God
because of His bad imitators. And they see and hear
nothing of the creation round about them and in them
that glows, and surges, and glitters, and is born anew with
every moment. All they do is go to the theatre, read
poetry and novels, and grimace like the characters they
find in them, and then say to God's real creations: How
commonplace!—The Greeks knew what they were about
when they told of Pygmalion's statue, come to life, but
unable to bear children.
    Danton. And artists handle nature like the painter
David. In September when they threw the murdered
bodies out of La Force onto the streets, he went around
cold-bloodedly drawing them and said: "I'm snatching the
last spasms of life from these scoundrels."

DANTON *is called out.*

Camille. What do *you* say, Lucille?

Lucille. Nothing; I'd rather watch you talk.

Camille. Do you listen to what I say?

Lucille. Well, of course!

Camille. Am I right? Do you know what I was talking about?

Lucille. No, not really.

DANTON *returns.*

Camille. What is it?

Danton. The Committee of Public Safety has just now ordered my arrest. I've been warned and offered a place of refuge.—It seems they want my head; for all I care they can have it. I'm disgusted with this bungled work. I wish they *would* take it. What difference does it make? I'll know how to die bravely; it's easier than living.

Camille. Danton, there's still time!

Danton. No—but I would never have thought that——

Camille. Your damned laziness!

Danton. I'm not lazy; I'm tired; even the soles of my feet burn.

Camille. Where will you go?

Danton. I wish I knew!

Camille. I'm asking you seriously: where?

Danton. For a walk, my friend, for a walk. [*He goes out.*

Lucille. Oh, Camille!

Camille. Don't worry, my love!

Lucille. When I think that this head—yours—! Oh, Camille! Tell me I'm not talking sense—please—that I don't know what I'm talking about!

Camille. Don't worry—Danton and I are two different people.

Lucille. The earth is broad and there are many things upon it—why should they want just this? Who would take him from me? It would be wicked. What would they want him for?

Camille. How many times must I tell you, you needn't worry. I spoke with Robespierre yesterday—he was friendly to me. Things are a bit strained at the moment, that's true; our points of view are different, nothing more!

Lucille. You must go to him.

Camille. We sat together on the same school bench. He was always gloomy and alone. I was the only one who ever sought him out and made him laugh at times. He has always shown me a great deal of affection. All right, I'll go.

Lucille. So quickly, my love? Go on! No, come here! There [*She kisses him.*], and there. Go now! Go!

CAMILLE *goes off.*

Lucille. These are terrible times. But that's how it is. What is there we can do? We simply must get hold of ourselves. [*Sings.*]

Parting, oh, parting, oh, parting,
Who'd ever have thought we must part?

Why should that of all things have occurred to me just now? I don't like the way it came of its own accord.—As he went out, it seemed to me that he could never come back again, that he had to go farther and farther from me. —How empty the room is, just all of a sudden! The windows open as if a dead man had been laid out in here. I can't bear this place any longer.   [*She goes off.*

SCENE IV—*An open field*

DANTON. I'll go no farther. Why should I disturb this silence with the rustling of my footsteps and the sound of my breath. [*He sits down; after a pause.*] I was told once of a sickness that wipes out our memory. Death must be something like that. And then at times I hope that perhaps death is even more powerful and wipes away everything. If only it were true!—I'd run like a Christian then to rescue my enemy—my memory, that is.—This place should be safe; for my memory if not for me; but the grave should give me safety, at least it will make me forget. The grave kills memory. But back there, in Paris, memory kills *me*. I or it? Which shall it be? It's an easy choice. [*He rises and looks back whence he came.*]—I'm flirting with death. It's rather amusing to make eyes at

im from a distance.—Actually I should laugh at the
vhole business. There's a sense of permanence in me that
ays: tomorrow and the day after, and so on and on, will
•e no different from today. It's a meaningless alarm to
righten me. They'd never dare!   [*He goes off.*

SCENE V—*A room—night*

)ANTON [*at the window*]. Will it never stop? Will the
ight never soften and the noise die away? Will it never
•e dark again and still so that we needn't look at and
sten to each other's ugly sins?—September!

Julie [*calls from within*]. Danton! Danton!

Danton. Yes?

Julie [*enters*]. Why are you calling out?

Danton. Was I?

Julie. You talked about ugly sins, and then you groaned:
eptember!

Danton. Did I? I? No, it wasn't I who spoke; I was
carcely thinking such things, they were scarcely more
han quiet, secret thoughts.

Julie. You're trembling, Danton!

Danton. Why shouldn't I tremble, with the walls chat-
ering as they are; if my body is so gone to pieces that my
houghts go astray and start speaking through lips of
tone? It's a strange thing.

Julie. Georges, Georges.

Danton. Yes, Julie, it's strange indeed. I'd rather never
hink again, if my thoughts are going to speak out for me.
There are thoughts, Julie, that are meant for no one's
ars. It's not good when they cry out like newborn chil-
ren; it's not good.

Julie. God keep you in your right mind!—Georges,
Georges, do you recognize me?

Danton. Why shouldn't I? You're a human being and
ou're a woman and my wife, and the earth has five
ontinents: Europe, Asia, Africa, America, Australia, and
wo times two makes four. You see, I'm in my right mind.
You say there was a cry: September. You did say that,
idn't you?

Julie. Yes, Danton, I heard it through all the rooms.

Danton. As I went to the window—. [*He looks out.*] How quiet the city is, it's lights are out. . . .

Julie. A child's crying near by.

Danton. As I went to the window—there cried and shrieked through all the streets: September!

Julie. You were dreaming, Danton. Calm yourself!

Danton. Dreaming? Yes, I dreamed; but that was something else. I'll tell you in a moment—my memory's so bad right now—in a moment! Yes, I have it now: the globe of the world writhed under me as it leapt from its course; I had grabbed hold of it like a wild horse, I clutched at its mane with giant arms and dug into its ribs, my head turned aside, my hair streaming across the abyss, and I dragged along. Then I cried out in terror, and I woke up. I walked to the window—and then I heard it, Julie.— What does it want from me? Why *that* word? What have I to do with it? Why does it stretch its bloody hands at me? I never struck at it.—Oh, help me, Julie, my mind is numb and dull! What happened in September, Julie?

Julie. The kings were within forty hours of Paris . . .

Danton. The fortresses fallen, the aristocrats in the city . . .

Julie. The Republic was lost.

Danton. Yes, lost. We couldn't leave the enemy at our back, we would have been fools: two enemies on a single plank; we or they, the stronger always pushes the weaker down—it was only fair, wasn't it?

Julie. Yes, yes.

Danton. We killed them—but it wasn't murder; it was war, civil war.

Julie. You saved the country.

Danton. Yes, I saved it; it was self-defense, we had no choice. That Man on the Cross made it easy for Himself: "It must needs be that offenses come; but woe to that man by whom the offense cometh." That *must*! That *must* was *mine*! Who will curse the hand on which that curse of *must* has fallen? Who spoke that *must*? Who. What is this in us that lies, whores, steals, and murders?— What are we but puppets, manipulated on wires by unknown powers? We are nothing, nothing in ourselves: we are the swords that spirits fight with—except no one sees the hands—just as in fairy tales.—I feel calmer now.

Julie. Really calm, my love?

Danton. Yes, Julie. Come—to bed!

SCENE VI—*Street in front of* DANTON'*s house*

SIMON. CITIZEN-SOLDIERS.

SIMON. How goes the night?

First Citizen. What do you mean "how goes the night"?

Simon. How far has the night gone?

First Citizen. As far as between sunset and sunrise.

Simon. You rogue, what time is it?

First Citizen. Look at your timepiece: it's time for perpendiculars to sprout between the bedsheets.

Simon. Forward, Citizens, forward! We must answer for it with our heads! Dead or alive! Watch for his strong arms! I'll lead you on, Citizens! Make way for Freedom!— See to my wife! I shall bequeath her a ring of walnuts for her table.

First Citizen. A ring of walnuts? She has her fill of nuts all right, and on the table, too!

Simon. Forward, Citizens, we shall put the country in our debt!

Second Citizen. I'd rather we were in the country's debt! For all the holes we made in people's bodies, the holes in our pants have stayed as big as ever.

First Citizen. What are you after, you want your fly sewn up? Ha! Ha! Ha!

The Others. Ha! Ha! Ha!

Simon. Away! Away!

They force their way into DANTON'*s house.*

SCENE VII—*The National Convention*

A group of DEPUTIES

LEGENDRE. Will this slaughter of Deputies never end? What man can be safe if Danton falls?

A Deputy. What can we do?

Another. He must be heard here in the Convention. It can't fail; what can they charge him with to his own face?

Another. That's impossible. There's a decree forbidding it.

Legendre. It must either be withdrawn or an exception made. I'll make the motion; I count on your support.

The President. The session is opened.

Legendre [ascends the tribune]. I have learned that four members of the National Convention were arrested during the night just past. I know that Danton was one of them; I do not know the names of the others. But be they who they may be, I demand that they be heard here in the Convention. Citizens, I declare this to you here and now: I hold Danton to be as innocent as myself, and I do not believe that any accusation can be brought against me. I have no thought of attacking any member of the Committees of Public Safety or General Security, but I am in possession of well-established reasons which make me fear that for certain private hatreds and private passions Liberty may be denied some particular men who have served her most greatly. That man, who in 1792 saved France by virtue of his private energy, that man deserves to be heard; he must be allowed to defend himself if he is to be accused of high treason. *[A great commotion breaks out.]*

Some Voices. We support Legendre's motion.

A Deputy. We are here in the name of the people; we cannot be deprived of our places except by the will of our voters.

Another. Your words smell like corpses; you've stolen them from Girondist mouths. You want privileges? The ax of the law hovers over every head.

Another. We cannot allow our Committees to send our own legislators to the guillotine without the protection of the law.

Another. Crime knows no protection. Only royal criminals find protection—on the throne.

Another. Only thieves ask for such protection.

Another. Only murderers fail to recognize it.

Robespierre. Such disorder, which has been unknown to this Assembly for some time, suggests to me that there is a matter of some import under discussion here. It is to be decided today whether several men are to score a victory over their country.—How is it possible that you are able to deny your principles to the extent of granting today to a few individuals what but recently you refused to such men as Chabot, Delaunai, and Fabre? What distinction is there in favor of these men? And why should I be concerned with the complimentary speeches which people pay themselves and their friends? We have had experiences enough to show us what they are worth. We do not ask whether a man has accomplished this or that patriotic action; we are concerned with his entire political career.—Legendre appears not to know the names of the others arrested; yet the whole Convention knows them. How is it Legendre appears not to know this? Because he knows well enough that only shamelessness can defend Lacroix. He has named only Danton, because he believes that a special privilege attaches itself to this name. No, we will have nothing of privileges, we will have nothing of idols! [*Applause.*]

What distinction has Danton over Lafayette, Dumouriez, and Brissot; over Fabre, Chabot, and Hébert? What could be said of them that cannot also be said of him? Did you spare them as well? What has earned him this advantage over his fellow citizens? Perhaps because certain deceived individuals, and others who did not allow themselves to be deceived, ranged themselves about him in order to fall into the arms of power and fortune as a result of his success. The more he has betrayed the trust of those patriots who believed in him, just that much more vigorous must he find the strength of all those who love Liberty. They will try to inspire you with fear at the misuse of a power which you yourself have exercised. They cry out about the despotism of the Committees, as though the confidence which the people placed in you, and which you in turn have handed over to these Committees, were not sufficient guarantee of your own patriotism. They pretend as if we were all trembling. But I tell you, whoever trembles at this moment, he is guilty; because innocence never trembles in face of public vigilance. [*General applause.*]

They have tried to frighten me as well; they have given me to understand that the danger that threatened Danton might not stop until it reached me. They wrote me that Danton's friends held me besieged, in the thought that a recollection of a former association and a blind trust in some simulated virtues might convince me to mitigate my zeal and passion in regard to Liberty. And so I declare this to you: there is nothing will blunt my purpose, even though Danton's danger become my own. We all have need of a bit of courage and some greatness of soul. Only criminals and base spirits are afraid to see their kind fall at their side; for without the safety in numbers of their accomplices, they would stand revealed in the light of truth. And if there are such spirits in this Assembly, then there are also those who are heroic. The number of scoundrels is not great; we have very few heads to let fall, and our country is saved. [*Applause.*]

I demand that Legendre's motion be rejected.

The DEPUTIES *rise in a body as a sign of their general agreement.*

Saint-Just. It appears in this Assembly that there are a number of sensitive ears that cannot endure mention of the word "blood." A number of general observations might convince them that we are no more gruesome than Nature or Time. Nature follows its laws quietly and unresistingly; Man is destroyed when he comes into conflict with them. An alteration in the composition of air, a flare-up of the tellurian fires, a fluctuation in the balance of bodies of water, and an epidemic, a volcanic eruption, a flood— each of these can bury thousands. What is the result? An insignificant, and on the whole scarcely noticeable, alteration of physical Nature, which might almost have passed without a trace, were it not for the bodies in its path.—I ask you now: Shall the moral universe take more consideration in its revolutions than the physical universe? Shall an idea not have equal rights with the

law of physics in regard to annihilating that which op-
poses it? Moreover, shall an event which changes the
entire configuration of the moral universe, and by that
I mean humanity, not be allowed the shedding of blood?
The forces that move the universe make use of our arms
in the world of the spirit just as in the physical world
they make use of volcanoes and floods. What matter
whether they die of an epidemic or of the Revolution?—
The strides of humanity are slow, one can count them
only in centuries; behind each one rise the graves of
generations. In order to arrive at the most basic principles and discoveries, millions have had to sacrifice their
lives along the way. Is it not understandable then that in
an age where the pace of history is increased, all the
more people should find themselves—out of breath?—
We will conclude, then, quickly and simply: Since all
men were created under the same circumstances, then all
men are equal, allowing for the differences which Nature
herself has imposed. Each man, therefore, is entitled to
the same benefits, but no man to any special privileges,
whether he be an individual or a smaller or larger class
of individuals.—Every link in the chain of this argument
translated into reality has cost human lives. The four-
teenth of July, the tenth of August, the thirty-first of
May—these are its punctuation marks. It has required
four years to make of the idea a fact; under normal circumstances it would have required a century, with generations serving as punctuation marks. Is it so astounding
then that the great flood of the revolution tosses up its
dead at every bend and turn?—We still have certain
conclusions to append to our proposition; are a couple of
hundred bodies to hinder us from doing so? Moses led
his people through the Red Sea and into the desert, till
the old corrupt generation had annihilated itself—and
only then did he found his new city. Legislators! Al-
though we have neither the Red Sea nor the desert, we
do have the war and the guillotine. The Revolution is
like the daughters of Pelias: they cut humanity in pieces
to make it young again. Humanity will rise from this
caldron of blood, as the earth once rose from the waters

of the Deluge, with arms strong as though created anew. [*Long, sustained applause. Several* DEPUTIES *rise in enthusiasm.*]

We herewith summon forth all the enemies of tyranny, whether in Europe or on the face of the entire earth, we summon these secret men, who bear the dagger of Brutus under their cloaks, to join with us and share this moment of triumph!

The SPECTATORS *and the* DEPUTIES *strike up the* Marseillaise.

ACT THREE

SCENE I—*The Luxembourg. A room with* PRISONERS.

CHAUMETTE, MERCIER, HÉRAULT-SÉCHELLES, *and other* PRISONERS

CHAUMETTE [*tugs at* PAINE's *sleeve*]. Paine, listen—it could be the way you say; I was almost sure of it a while back. I have a headache—help me a little with some of your arguments; I feel very bad today.

Paine. All right, Anaxagoras, I'll help you with your catechism.—*There is no God,* because: either God created the world or He did not. If He did not, then the world contains its own first principle, and there is no God because God can only be God in so far as He contains the first principle of all things. Now, however, God cannot have created the world: for either the creation is eternal with God, or it has a beginning. If the latter is true, then God must have created it at a certain point in Time; and God must also, having rested for an eternity, have suddenly become active, and must therefore have suffered a change in Himself, which made Him subject to the concept of Time, both of which conflict with the nature of God's being. Therefore God cannot have created the world. And since we know quite certainly that the world, or at least our ego, exists, and that, according to what I have said before, it must also have its first principle either in itself or in something else, which is not God, it therefore follows that there can be no God. *Quod erat demonstrandum.*

Chaumette. Yes . . . yes—that makes it all so clear again; thank you!

Mercier. Just a minute, Paine! But what if creation *is* eternal?

Paine. Then it's no longer a creation, for then it is one with God, or an Attribute of Him, as Spinoza says; then God is in all things, in you, my friend, in our Anaxagoras here, and in me. That wouldn't be so bad, but you must agree that it doesn't say much for the Divine Majesty when the Good Lord God has to have a toothache or the clap or be buried alive with each one of us, or at least have the very unpleasant concept of it.

Mercier. But there must be a reason for it somewhere.

Paine. Who says otherwise? But who claims that this basic principle has to be what we call God, that is, what we think of as perfection? Do you take the world to be perfect?

Mercier. No.

Paine. Then how would you explain an imperfect effect proceeding from a perfect cause?—Voltaire dared offend God just as little as he did the kings; that's why he did it. If a man has only his reasoning and doesn't know how to use it, or doesn't dare, then he is nothing but a blunderer.

Mercier. Let me ask you this: can a perfect cause have a perfect effect, that is, can something perfect create something imperfect? Isn't it impossible, because that which is created cannot contain within itself its own first principle, which, as you say, the perfect does contain?

Chaumette. No, no! Keep quiet!

Paine. Calm yourself, philosopher!—You're quite right; but why should God *have to* create at all? If He can create only the imperfect, then it were best He leave well alone. Isn't it rather a weakness in our humanity that we can only conceive of God as working? Simply because *we* must always be moving and bustling about to convince ourselves of our existence, must we also attribute this miserable need to God? Why must we, if our spirit is sunk in a being harmoniously at rest in itself in eternal blessedness, assume at once that it stretches out its finger across the table and kneads men out of dough? We always whisper in one another's ears that it's out of a boundless need for love. Must we go through all this merely to make ourselves sons of God? I'd just as soon have a less imposing Father; at least I wouldn't be able to say of Him that He let me be raised below His station in a pigsty or galleys. First do away with the imperfect, and then you can demonstrate God; Spinoza tried it. One can deny evil, but not pain; only reasoning can prove God, feeling rebels against it. Consider this, Anaxagoras: why do I suffer? That is the very bedrock of atheism. The least quiver of pain, in even the smallest of atoms, makes a rent in the curtain of your creation from top to bottom.

Mercier. And what of morality?

Paine. First you prove God from morality, then morality from God! What do you want with this morality of yours? Properly considered I don't know whether there is such a thing as good or evil, and for that reason I have no need to change my way of life. I act according to what my nature tells me; whatever is suitable to it is good for me and I do it, and whatever is repulsive to it is evil and I do not do it and I defend myself against it when it comes my way. You can stay virtuous, as they say, and defend yourself against so-called vice without despising your enemies, which is a very sad feeling.

Chaumette. True, very true!

Hérault-Séchelles. But, my good Anaxagoras, one might also say: since God is all things, then He must also be His own opposite, that is, perfect and imperfect, good and evil, happy and unhappy; the result of course would be nil, each side would cancel out the other, we would come to nothing.—Be glad you've come through victorious; you can continue worshiping Madame Momoro as Nature's masterwork; she's at least given you a crown of rosebuds in your groin.

Chaumette. I thank you, gentlemen. I thank you most heartily!   [*He goes off.*

Paine. He's still not certain. Before it's all over he'll have had Extreme Unction, set his feet toward Mecca, and been circumcised, so as to leave no way unexplored.

DANTON, LACROIX, CAMILLE, *and* PHILIPPEAU *are led in.*

Hérault-Séchelles [*rushes to* DANTON *and embraces him*]. Good morning! Or, good night, I should say. I can't ask you *how* you've slept, but: how *will* you sleep?

Danton. Very well; I shall go to bed laughing.

Mercier [*to* PAINE]. These great Danes with wings of doves! He's the evil genius of the Revolution; he dared defy his mother, but she was stronger than he.

Paine. His death is as great a misfortune as his life.

Lacroix [*to* DANTON]. I didn't expect you would be here so soon.

Danton. Yes, I knew; I was warned.

Lacroix. And you said nothing?

Danton. To what? Isn't a stroke the best of all deaths? Or would you rather suffer first in sickness? And—well, you see, I didn't think they would dare. [*To* HÉRAULT-SÉCHELLES.] I'd rather lie *in* the earth than rub corns on my feet *on* it. I prefer it as a pillow rather than as a footstool.

Hérault-Séchelles. At least we won't have calluses on our fingers when we stroke the cheeks of our good lady Decay.

Camille [*to* DANTON]. Why trouble yourself? Your tongue could hang out as far as your neck, but you could never lick the sweat of death from your brow.—Oh, Lucille! What a terrible thing this is!

The PRISONERS *throng about the new arrivals.*

Danton [*to* PAINE]. What you have done for the good of your country, I have tried to do for mine. I wasn't quite as fortunate; they're sending me to the scaffold. For my sake I hope I don't stumble.

Mercier [*to* DANTON]. You're drowning in the blood of the twenty-two Girondins.

A Prisoner [*to* HÉRAULT-SÉCHELLES]. So the power of the people and the power of Reason are one, uh?

Another [*to* CAMILLE]. Well, General Procurator of Street Lamps, your improvement in the lighting of streets hasn't made France any brighter.

Another. Let him alone! Wasn't he the one who

talked about mercy? [*He embraces* CAMILLE; *a number of others follow his example.*]

Philippeau. We are priests who have prayed with the dying; we have become infected and are dying of the same epidemic.

Several Voices. The blow that strikes you down strikes us as well.

Camille. Gentlemen, I very much regret that our efforts have proved so useless; I go to the scaffold now, because my eyes grew moist at the fate of a few unfortunate men.

SCENE II—A *room*

FOUQUIER-TINVILLE. HERMAN

FOUQUIER. Everything ready?

Herman. It won't be easy; of course if Danton weren't among them it would be.

Fouquier. He's also going to have to lead the dance.

Herman. You know he'll frighten the jury; he's the scarecrow of the Revolution.

Fouquier. The jury must will it.

Herman. There is a way, but it's not quite according to the letter of the law.

Fouquier. Speak up!

Herman. Instead of drawing the jury by lots, we'll pick out those we can depend on.

Fouquier. It'll have to work.—That will make a good running fire. There are nineteen of them. A cleverly mixed bunch. The four forgers, then a few bankers and foreigners. That will make a spicy Tribunal. The people need something of the sort.—All right then, reliable people! Who, for example?

Herman. Leroi. He's so stone-deaf he won't hear a word of the defense; Danton can shout himself hoarse.

Fouquier. Excellent. Go on.

Herman. Vilatte and Lumière. One of them never gets his hand off the bottle and the other one's always sleeping; they won't open their mouths except to say "Guilty." —Girard has a rule of honor that no one escapes the Tribunal once he's appeared before it. And Renaudin——

Fouquier. Why Renaudin? He once helped a couple of priests get through our hands.

Herman. Don't get excited! He came to me a few days ago and demanded that the condemned be bled a bit before their execution, to make them a little less spirited; he was annoyed by their generally defiant attitude.

Fouquier. I see—very good. Then I shall rely on you!

Herman. I'll see to it!

SCENE III—*The Conciergerie. A corridor*

LACROIX, DANTON, MERCIER, *and other* PRISONERS *pace to and fro.*

LACROIX [*to a* PRISONER]. These poor wretches!

The Prisoner. Don't you know? Paris is a slaughter-house! Don't the carts rolling to the guillotine tell you as much!

Mercier. Don't you know, Lacroix, that Equality swings its sickle over all heads without distinction? The lava of the Revolution flows on! The guillotine makes good Republicans! The galleries applaud and the Romans rub their hands together in delight. But what they don't hear in every one of the words spoken is the death rattle of another victim.—Follow up your words sometime to where they become human forms. Take a good look around you, you see here everything that you've said: a faithful translation of your own words. These miserable creatures, their executioners, and the guillotine are your speeches come to life. You erect your systems like Bajazet his pyramids—from the heads of men.

Danton. You're right—everything we build today is of human flesh. That's the curse of our age. And now my own body will become a building block.—It's exactly a year now since I created the Revolutionary Tribunal. I ask both God and man to forgive me that; I wanted to prevent another September Massacre, I hoped to rescue the innocent, but this long-drawn-out murder with its formalities is even more terrible and just as inevitable. I had hoped, gentlemen, to save you all from this place.

Mercier. Oh, we'll get out of it, all right.

Danton. And now I'm here *with* you; heaven only knows how it will end.

SCENE IV—*The Revolutionary Tribunal*

HERMAN [*to* DANTON]. Citizen, your name.

Danton. The Revolution gives me my name. My place of dwelling will soon be in nothingness and my name in the Pantheon of History.

Herman. Danton, the Convention accuses you of conspiring with Mirabeau, with Dumouriez, with Orléans, with the Girondists, with foreigners, and the faction of Louis XVII.

Danton. My voice, which I have so often raised in the people's cause, will find little difficulty in refuting this wrongful accusation. If the wretches who have accused me should care to appear, I will cover them with shame. And if the Committee should care to appear, then I will answer, for otherwise I will not. I have need of them both as accusers and as witnesses. If they would be so kind.—Moreover, what concern have I with you and your decisions? I have told you once already that my asylum will soon be nothingness; life has become a burden, you may tear it from me, I long to be rid of it.

Herman. Danton, audacity is the mark of the criminal, calmness that of the innocent.

Danton. Private audacity is indeed blameworthy, but that national audacity which I have so often manifested, with which I have so often fought for Freedom, is the most meritorious of all virtues. That is my audacity; it is the audacity that serves me here in face of my pitiable accusers, and in the best interests of the Republic. How should I be calm when I find myself so basely slandered? Do you expect a revolutionary like me to defend himself dispassionately? Men of my stamp are inestimable in Revolutions, the Spirit of Freedom hovers upon our brows. [*Signs of applause from among the* SPECTATORS.] I am accused of having conspired with Mirabeau, with Dumouriez, with Orléans, of having debased myself at the feet of miserable despots. I am required to answer your inescapable and inflexible justice.—You, Saint-Just, will be answerable to posterity for this blasphemy against me!

Herman. I require you to answer calmly; you might take Marat's example; he approached his judges with awe.

Danton. You have placed my entire life in your hands; I think it has a right to rise up and meet you face on; I will bury you under the weight of every one of my accomplishments.—I am not proud of this. It is destiny commands our actions, but it chooses only powerful natures for its instruments.—I declared war on the monarchy on the Champ de Mars, on the tenth of August I deposed it, and on the twenty-first of September I killed it, and to all the kings of Europe I threw down as my gauntlet the head of a king. [*Repeated signs of applause. He takes up the Bill of Indictment.*]

When I look at this shameful document my whole being trembles. Who, then, are those men who had to force Danton to appear on that memorable day, the tenth of August? Who, then, are those privileged beings from whom he borrowed his strength?—I demand that my accusers appear in front of me! And I am in my right mind when I make this demand. I will unmask these repulsive villains and cast them back into the nothingness whence they ought never to have crept.

Herman [*ringing the bell*]. Do you hear this bell?

Danton. The voice of a man defending his honor and his life must cry louder than your petty bell.—In September I gorged the young brood of this Revolution on the finely chopped flesh of the aristocracy. My voice forged weapons for the people out of the aristocracy's gold and riches. My voice was the hurricane that buried the satellites of despotism under waves of bayonets. [*Loud applause.*]

Herman. You have strained your voice, Danton, you are too violently moved. You shall conclude your defense the next time, you are in need of rest.—The session is adjourned.

Danton. You know Danton now—·yet a few hours and he shall slumber in the arms of glory.

SCENE V—*The Luxembourg. A cell*

General DILLON. LAFLOTTE. A JAILER

DILLON. You, stop shining your nose in my face. Ha, ha, ha!

Laflotte. And close your mouth, too; that sickle-moon of a nose has a halo around it from all your stink. Ha, ha, ha!

Jailer. Ha, ha, ha! Do you gentlemen think my nose is bright enough to read by? [*He points to a paper in his hand.*]

Dillon. Give it here!

Jailer. I'm at ebb tide now, sir, with the cost of keeping my moon lighted.

Laflotte. But your pants look more like flood tide.

Jailer. Yes, sir, the practice provokes water, too. [*To* DILLON.] My moon hides from your sun, sir; you must give me something to make it glow again if you want to read, sir.

Dillon. There, you rogue! Now get out!

He gives the JAILER *money. The* JAILER *goes off.*

Dillon [*reads*]. "Danton has roused the Tribunal, shaken the jury, and caused the people to grow restless. The crowd was extraordinary. The people thronged around the Palace of Justice all the way to the bridge across the Seine. A handful of gold, a push——" Hm! Hm! [*He paces to and fro, pouring himself a drink now and then from a bottle.*] If I could get one foot outside this prison, I'd never give in to this slaughter. Just one foot out!

Laflotte. And onto the cart? It's all one.

Dillon. Do you really think so? I see a few steps' difference, wide enough to be covered up by the bodies of the Committee. The time has come for decent people to lift up their heads.

Laflotte [*to himself*]. To make it easier to cut them off. Come on, old man; a few more glasses and you'll be floating.

Dillon. The scoundrels, the fools, they'll guillotine themselves in the end. [*He walks quickly back and forth.*]

Laflotte [*aside*]. One could learn to love life properly

again, like his own child, if he could give himself life. It isn't often a man can commit incest with chance and become his own father. Father and child at the same time. A cozy little Oedipus!

Dillon. You don't feed the people with corpses! Danton's and Camille's wives ought to throw money to the people, that's better than heads any day.

Laflotte [*aside*]. On second thought, I don't think I'll tear out my eyes like Oedipus; I might need them to weep for the good general.

Dillon. The idea of laying their hands on Danton! Who can be safe after this? But fear will unite them.

Laflotte [*aside*]. He's lost for sure. What does it matter then if I clamber over a corpse to get out of this grave?

Dillon. If I could get just one foot out of this prison! I'd find enough people, old soldiers, Girondists, ex-nobles; we'd break open the prisons—we must come to terms with the prisoners.

Laflotte [*aside*]. Of course it does smell a bit of villainy. But what does that matter? I'd like to try my hand at that for a change, too; I've been too one-sided up till now. It could give one pangs of conscience, but that's a change, too; it's not so unpleasant to smell your own stink.—The prospect of the guillotine has grown a bit tedious by now; imagine having to wait so long for a thing like that! I've rehearsed the scene in my mind twenty times over. I've lost all interest in it; it's become rather common.

Dillon. We must get a letter through to Danton's wife.

Laflotte [*aside*]. And then—no, I'm not afraid of death, it's the pain. There's nobody can tell me it won't hurt. Of course they say it only takes a moment; but pain always measures with a more delicate scale. No! Pain is the only sin, and suffering the only vice; I'll stay virtuous.

Dillon. Listen, Laflotte, where's that fellow gone? I have money here, and I've got to use it. We must strike while we still can; I've worked it all out.

Laflotte. Yes, at once, at once! I know the jailer; I'll talk to him. You can count on me, General; we'll get out of this prison all right—[*To himself, going out.*] only to be thrown into another: myself into the big one they call the world, he into the small one known as the grave.

SCENE VI—*The Committee of Public Safety*

SAINT-JUST, BARÈRE, COLLOT D'HERBOIS, BILLAUD-VARENNES

BARÈRE. What does Fouquier write?

Saint-Just. The second hearing's over. The prisoners demand the appearance of more members of the Convention and of the Committee of Public Safety; they've appealed to the people because of the refusal to allow witnesses. He says the excitement is indescribable.—Danton's been parodying Jupiter and shaking his locks.

Collot. The easier for the executioner to grasp him by them.

Barère. I don't think we'd better show ourselves, the fishwives and ragpickers might find us somewhat less imposing.

Billaud-Varennes. These people have an instinct for being trodden on, even if only with looks; they like insolent faces. They're more irritating than a coat-of-arms; they have the stamp of the aristocracy's contempt for humanity. And one who doesn't like to be looked up and down should help to smash them in.

Barère. He's like the Horned Siegfried, the blood of the September Massacre has made him invulnerable.—What does Robespierre say?

Saint-Just. He only *acts* as if he had something to say.—The jury must declare itself sufficiently informed and end the hearings.

Barère. That's impossible—it would never work.

Saint-Just. We must get rid of them at any cost, even if we have to strangle them with our bare hands! "Dare!" Danton mustn't have taught us that word for nothing. The Revolution won't stumble over its own corpses; but if Danton stays alive he'll grab her by the skirt, and from what I see in his face he's liable to rape Liberty herself.

SAINT-JUST *is called out.* A JAILER *enters.*

Jailer. Some of the prisoners in Sainte Pélagie are dying, sir; they asked for a doctor.

Billaud-Varennes. That won't be necessary; just that much less work for the executioner.

Jailer. Some of the women are pregnant.

Billaud-Varennes. Excellent; we won't need coffins for the children.

Barère. Every consumptive aristocrat saves the Tribunal a sitting. And every bit of medicine would be counter-revolutionary.

Collot [*takes a paper*]. A petition! A woman's name!

Barère. Probably one of those forced to choose between the guillotine and a Jacobin's bed. They die like Lucretia, at the loss of their honor—but somewhat later than the Roman matron: in childbed, perhaps, or of cancer, or old age.—It might not be so unpleasant to drive a Tarquin out of the virtuous republic of a virgin.

Collot. She's too old. Madame wants to die; she knows how to express herself: prison lies upon her like the lid of a coffin; she's been there four weeks. The answer's easy: [*He reads as he writes.*] "Citizeness, you have not yet wished long enough for death."   [*The* JAILER *goes off.*

Barère. Well said! And yet, Collot, I don't think it's proper for the guillotine to begin laughing; as it is, the people aren't afraid of it any more; we shouldn't get too familiar about it.

SAINT-JUST *re-enters.*

Saint-Just. I've just received a letter of denunciation. A conspiracy's under way in the prison; a young man named Laflotte discovered it. He was in the same cell as Dillon, and Dillon became drunk and talked.

Barère. So he simply cuts his throat with his bottle; that's happened often enough.

Saint-Just. The wives of Danton and Camille are to throw money to the people, Dillon will escape, the prisoners be freed, and the Convention blown up.

Barère. Fairy tales!

Saint-Just. These fairy tales will send them to sleep, all right. I have the report here; add to that the impudence of the accused, the people's dissatisfaction, the confusion of the jury—I'll make a report.

Barère. Yes, Saint-Just, you go on spinning out your sentences, with every comma the stroke of a sword, and every period a chopped-off head!

Saint-Just. The Convention must decree that the Tribunal continue the trial without interruption and that every prisoner who fails to show due respect toward the court or creates a disturbance will be excluded from the hearings.

Barère. You do have an instinct for the revolutionary! It all sounds quite moderate, but it's also bound to succeed. They'll never be able to keep themselves down, and Danton's bound to let go.

Saint-Just. I'm counting on your support. There are people in the Convention who are as sick as Danton and afraid of being served the same cure. They've regained courage and will start complaining about unconstitutional procedures——

Barère [*interrupting him*]. And I'll tell them that's what happened to the Roman Consul who uncovered Catiline's conspiracy and had the criminals executed on the spot—they complained about unconstitutional procedures then, too. And who were his accusers?

Collot [*with theatrical solemnity*]. Go, Saint-Just! The lava of the Revolution flows! Liberty shall suffocate with her embrace those weaklings who would lie within her lap; the majesty of the people shall appear in thunder and lightning like Jupiter to Semele and change them all to ashes. Go, Saint-Just, we will help you thrust your thunderbolt down upon the heads of these cowards!

[SAINT-JUST *goes off.*]

Barère. Did you hear him use the word "cure"? Next thing you know they'll be calling the guillotine a cure for syphilis. They're not fighting the moderates, they're fighting vice.

Billaud-Varennes. This is the first time we've disagreed.

Barère. Robespierre wants to turn the Revolution into a morals lecture hall, and the guillotine into a pulpit.

Billaud-Varennes. Or into a cushion to kneel on while praying.

Collot. And on which he'll finally lie rather than kneel.

Barère. That will be easy enough. The world will be

standing on its head when all the so-called rogues are
hanged by all the so-called righteous people.

Collot [to BARÈRE]. When are you coming to Clichy
again?

Barère. When the doctor's done with me.

Collot. Is it true that over the place there hangs a
comet, and that its scorching rays dry up the marrow of
your spinal column?

Billaud-Varennes. And soon the lovely fingers of that
Demaly will pull it from its sheath and make it hang
down like a pigtail behind your back.

Barère [shrugs his shoulders]. Hm! What can the virtuous know of such things!

Billaud-Varennes. The impotent pedant!

[BILLAUD-VARENNES *and* COLLOT *go off.*

Barère [alone]. The monsters!—"You have not yet
wished long enough for death!" These words should have
withered the tongue that spoke them.—And I?—When
the Septembrists broke into the prison, one of the prisoners seized a knife, joined with the assassins, thrust it into
the breast of a priest, and was saved! Who can blame him
for that? Shall I join with the assassins now, or sit on the
Committee of Public Safety? Shall I use the guillotine or
a pocketknife? The situation is the same, only the circumstances are more involved.—And being allowed to
murder one man, why not two, or three, or more? Where
does it end? It's like barleycorns! Do two make a pile, or
three, or four? How many? Come, my conscience, come,
my little chicken, come, chuck-chuck-chuck, here's your
feed!—But—I was never a prisoner. Yet I was under sus-
picion; that can mean only one thing: my death.

[*He goes off.*

SCENE VII—*The Conciergerie*

LACROIX, DANTON, PHILIPPEAU, CAMILLE

LACROIX. You were in good voice, Danton. If you had
taken such trouble for your life earlier it might be different now. Am I right? Especially now when death

comes so shamelessly close with her stinking breath, more
and more urgent?

Camille. Why can't death ravish a person and tear his
prize from our hot bodies with fighting and struggling!
But here with all these formalities, it's like marrying an
old woman, with contracts to sign, and witnesses to call,
and the Amen to be said, and then finally she crawls in
under the bedcovers with you with cold feet!

Danton. How I wish it *were* a fight, with arms and
teeth tearing and clutching! But it's as if I'd fallen into a
mill shaft, and my arms and legs were slowly and system-
atically being wrenched off by cold physical force. Imagine
being killed mechanically!

Camille. And then to lie there, alone, cold, stiff, in
the damp fog of decay—perhaps death will torture life
out of us fiber by fiber—perhaps we'll even be conscious
of the fact that we're falling to pieces!

Philippeau. Calm yourself, my friends. We're like the
autumn crocus that bears no seed until the winter's over.
The only difference between us and flowers being trans-
planted is that we stink a bit in the process. Is that so
bad?

Danton. What an edifying prospect! From one dunghill
to another! The divine theory of classes! From first we
move to second, from second to third, and so on and on.
I'm sick of school benches; I've sat calluses on my backside
like a monkey from sitting on them.

Philippeau. Then what do you want?

Danton. Peace.

Philippeau. Peace is in God.

Danton. Peace is in nothingness. Sink yourself into
something more peaceful than nothingness, and if the
ultimate peace is God, then God must be nothingness.
However, I'm an atheist. Damn whoever said: Something
cannot become nothing! The pitiable fact is that I *am
something!* Creation has spread itself so far that there is
nothing empty any more, multitudes everywhere. This is
the suicide of nothingness, creation is its wound, we its
drops of blood, and the world its grave in which it rots.
—Mad as that sounds, there is some truth in it.

Camille. The world is the Wandering Jew, and nothingness is death; but that's impossible. "Alas, alas, I cannot die!" as they sing in the old song.

Danton. We're all of us buried alive like kings in three or four layers of coffins: the sky, our houses, our shirts, and our coats. We scratch at the coffin lid for fifty long years. If only we could believe in annihilation! It would at least be a comfort. There's no hope in death; it's only a less complicated form of decay than life—that's the only difference!—But this is the very kind of decay that I've grown used to; the devil only knows how I'll adjust to another.—Oh, Julie! What if I go alone? What if I must leave her behind?—And even if I fell to pieces utterly, completely dissolved: I would always be a handful of tormented dust, no single atom of me could find rest except in her.—I can't die, no, I can't die. We must roar; they must tear every drop of life's blood from my body.

SCENE VIII—A *room*

FOUQUIER. AMAR. VOULAND

Fouquier. I don't know what to answer them any more; they're demanding a commission be appointed.

Amar. We've got the scoundrels now: here's what you've been wanting. [*He hands* FOUQUIER *a paper.*] The decree from Saint-Just.

Vouland. That should satisfy them.

Fouquier. Yes, we needed this.

Amar. Let's get this settled and out of the way for them *and* for us.

SCENE IX—*The Revolutionary Tribunal*

DANTON. The Republic is in danger and knows nothing of it! We appeal to the people; my voice is still strong enough to deliver a funeral oration for the Decemvirs.— I repeat: We demand the appointment of a commission; we have important matters to reveal. I shall withdraw to the citadel of Reason, and I shall break through with the artillery of Truth and cast down my enemies before me.

Signs of approval. FOUQUIER, AMAR, *and* VOULAND *enter.*

Fouquier. Silence in the name of the Republic and in the name of the law! The Convention decrees the following: In consideration of the fact that signs of mutiny have been detected in the prisons; in consideration of the fact that Danton's and Camille's wives are distributing money among the people, and that General Dillon is plotting to escape and place himself at the head of the insurgents in order to free the accused; and, finally, in consideration of the fact that the accused have gone out of their way to create disturbances and insult the Tribunal —the Tribunal is hereby empowered to continue the investigation without interruption, and to exclude from the trial any prisoner who shall fail to show the respect due to the law.

Danton. I ask all present whether we have defied the Tribunal, the people, or the National Convention?

Many Voices. No! No!

Camille. The beasts, they want to murder my Lucille!

Danton. The truth will be known one day. I see a great catastrophe overtaking France. It is dictatorship; it has torn off its veil, and carries its head high, and strides across our corpses. [*Pointing to* AMAR *and* VOULAND.] There you see the cowards, the murderers; you see there the ravens of the Committee of Public Safety!—I accuse Robespierre, Saint-Just, and their hangmen of high treason. They are out to suffocate the Republic in blood. The ruts made by the guillotine's carts are highways on which the enemies of France will surge into the heart of our country.—For how much longer must the footprints of Liberty be graves?—You ask for bread, and they toss you severed heads! You thirst, and they make you lap up blood from the guillotine's steps!

There is an uproar among the SPECTATORS,
cries of approval.

Many Voices. Long live Danton! Down with the Decemvirs!

The PRISONERS *are forcibly led away.*

SCENE X—*A square in front of the Palace of Justice*

A crowd

SEVERAL VOICES. Down with the Decemvirs! Long live Danton!

First Citizen. Yes, he's right! Heads instead of bread! Blood instead of wine!

Several Women. The guillotine's no mill, and the executioner's no baker! We want bread, bread!

Second Citizen. Danton's eating your bread. And his head will give it back to you. You can trust him.

First Citizen. Danton was with us on the tenth of August, Danton was with us in September. Where were the people who accused him?

Second Citizen. And Lafayette was with you at Versailles and still he was a traitor.

First Citizen. Who says that Danton's a traitor?

Second Citizen. Robespierre.

First Citizen. Then Robespierre's a traitor!

Second Citizen. Who says so?

First Citizen. Danton.

Second Citizen. Danton has nice clothes, Danton has a nice house, Danton has a nice wife; he bathes in Burgundy, eats game off silver dishes, sleeps with your wives and daughters when he's drunk.—Danton was as poor as you. Where did all this come from? The King bought it for him so Danton would save his crown. The Duke of Orléans gave it to him as a gift so Danton would steal the crown. The foreigners let him have it so Danton would betray you all.—What does Robespierre have? The virtuous Robespierre! You all know him.

All. Long live Robespierre! Down with Danton! Down with the traitors!

ACT FOUR

SCENE I—A room

JULIE. A BOY

JULIE. It's all over now. They trembled in front of him. They'll kill him because they're afraid. Go on! I've seen him for the last time; tell him I could never look at him as he is now. [*She gives him a lock of her hair.*] Here, take this to him and tell him that he won't have to go alone—he'll understand. And then come back to me quickly; I want to see him again—in your eyes.

SCENE II—A street

DUMAS. A CITIZEN

CITIZEN. How can they sentence so many innocent people to death after a trial like that?

Dumas. It does seem extraordinary; but these revolutionaries have an instinct about such things that others lack, and this instinct never misleads them.

Citizen. The instinct of a tiger.—You have a wife.

Dumas. Soon I will have had one.

Citizen. Then it's true?

Dumas. The Revolutionary Tribunal will pronounce our separation; the guillotine will divide us from bed and board.

Citizen. You're a monster!

Dumas. You fool! I suppose you admire Brutus?

Citizen. With all my heart.

Dumas. Must one be a Roman consul and able to hide his head in a toga in order to sacrifice his love to his country? The only difference between Brutus and myself is that I shall wipe my eyes with the sleeve of my red coat.

Citizen. But that's horrible!

Dumas. Go on, you wouldn't understand such things!

[*They go off.*

SCENE III—*The Conciergerie*

LACROIX, HÉRAULT-SÉCHELLES *on one bed,* DANTON *and*
CAMILLE *on another.*

LACROIX. The way your hair and nails grow in a place
like this makes you ashamed of yourself.

Hérault-Séchelles. I wish you'd be more careful, you
sneezed directly in my face!

Lacroix. And you, my friend, stop stepping on my
feet, my corns take exception to such treatment!

Hérault-Séchelles. And you've got lice, too.

Lacroix. Oh! I can hardly wait to be rid of the little
vermin!

Hérault-Séchelles. Well, good night! We'll have to see
how we get on with one another, there's little enough
room. Just don't scratch me with those nails in your sleep!
—There! Stop tearing at the shroud that way, it's cold
in here!

Danton. That's right, Camille, tomorrow we'll be worn-
out shoes that they'll throw in the lap of that beggar-
woman, earth.

Hérault-Séchelles. The cowhide that, according to Plato,
the angels make slippers from and grope about in on
the earth. It's all what you might expect.—Oh, Lucille!

Danton. Calm yourself, my boy!

Camille. How can I, Danton? How can you even think
I could? How can I? They can't even touch her, can
they? The beauty that shines from her precious body
can't be put out. Why, not even the earth would dare
bury her; it would arch itself over her body, the mist of
the grave would sparkle on her eyelashes like dew, crystals
would spring up like flowers around her limbs and bright
springs murmur her to sleep.

Danton. Go to sleep, my boy, go to sleep!

Camille. You know, Danton—just between us—it's a
terrible thing to die. It's all so useless. When it happens,
I'll want to steal just one last look from life in all its
beauty; yes, I'll keep my eyes open.

Danton. You'll keep them open anyway; our executioner

never holds one's eyes shut. Sleep is more merciful. Sleep, boy, sleep!

Camille. Lucille—I can imagine your kiss on my lips; every kiss becomes a dream; I'll close my eyes and dream —and hold them fast. . . .

Danton. Will the clock never stop! Every tick pushes the walls closer around me, till they're narrow as a coffin. —I read a story like that once when I was a child, it made my hair stand on end. Yes, when I was a child! It wasn't worth the trouble to fatten me up and keep me warm. Just another job for the gravediggers!—I feel as if I'd already begun to stink. My dear body, I shall hold my nose closed and imagine that you are a lovely woman, sweating and stinking a bit after a dance, and pay you compliments. We've had better times than this with one another. Tomorrow you'll be nothing but a broken fiddle with no more tunes to play. Tomorrow you'll be an empty bottle; I've emptied all the wine but I'm still not drunk and go sober to bed—they're lucky people who can still get drunk. Tomorrow you'll be a worn-out pair of pants; you'll be thrown in the wardrobe, and be eaten by moths, and then you can stink as much as you like.—Yes, it's useless! Of course it's miserable having to die. What does death do but mimic birth? We die as helpless and naked as newborn babes. And of course we get a shroud for swaddling clothes. What good will it do! We can whimper just as well in the grave as in the cradle.—Camille! He's sleeping. [*While bending over him.*] There's a dream between his lashes. I mustn't wipe that golden dew of sleep from his eyes. [*He rises and goes to the window.*] I won't be going alone: thank you, Julie! Still, I wish I could have died differently, without effort, like a star falling, or a note of music that breathes itself out, kissing itself with its own lips, like a ray of light burying itself in a sea of clear water.—The stars are scattered through the night like glistening teardrops; what a terrible grief must be behind the eyes that dropped them.

Camille. Oh! [*He has sat up, and gropes for the ceiling.*]

Danton. What is it, Camille?

Camille. Oh! Oh!

Danton [*shakes him*]. Are you trying to scratch the ceiling down?

Camille. Oh, it's you, it's you—hold me, please, talk to me!

Danton. Your whole body's trembling, there's sweat on your forehead.

Camille. Yes, it's you—and I'm here—yes! And this is my hand! Yes, I remember now.—Oh, Danton, it was terrible!

Danton. What was?

Camille. I was half between waking and sleeping. Then suddenly the ceiling disappeared, and the moon floated down into the room, close to me, it was thick, I held it with my arms. The sky came down on me with its lights, I pounded at it, I groped at the stars, I thrashed about like a man drowning under a layer of ice. Oh, Danton, it was terrible!

Danton. What you saw was the glow of the lamp on the ceiling.

Camille. It doesn't take much to make a man lose the little understanding he has left. I felt madness grasp me by the hair. [*He rises.*] I don't want to sleep any more, I don't want to go mad. [*He reaches for a book.*]

Danton. What are you reading?

Camille. Night Thoughts.

Danton. Why die twice! Give me *La Pucelle.* Why should I slide from life on my knees! I'd rather crawl from the bed of some merciful sister. Life's a whore; she fornicates with the whole world.

SCENE IV—*The Square in front of the Conciergerie*

A JAILER. Two CARTERS *with their carts.* WOMEN

JAILER. Who called you here?

First Carter. Here? I'm not called Here, that's a funny name.

Jailer. Blockhead, who gave you permission to come?

First Carter. Commission? I don't get commission— no more than ten sous a head.

Second Carter. The villain'd take the bread right out of my mouth.

First Carter. What do you mean: bread? [*Pointing toward the* PRISONERS' *window.*] There's food for worms.

Second Carter. My children are no better off than worms either, and they want their share, too. Oh, it's a bad trade we've got, even if we are the best carters.

First Carter. How do you mean?

Second Carter. Who's the best carter?

First Carter. The one that drives farthest and quickest.

Second Carter. You silly fool, how can you drive farther than driving people out of the world, and quicker than in fifteen minutes? It's exactly fifteen minutes from here to the guillotine.

Jailer. Hurry up, you lazy louts! Closer to the door! You girls get back!

First Carter. You stay there! You never go around a girl, you go through her.

Second Carter. Sure, I'll believe that: you'll find the road wide enough to take your horse and cart with you; but you'll be in quarantine when you get back out. [*They drive forward.*]

Second Carter [*to the* WOMEN]. What are you gawking at?

A Woman. Waiting to see our old customers.

Second Carter. You mean my cart will be a whorehouse? I'll have you know it's a respectable cart, the King and all the fine gentlemen from Paris rode in it to the scaffold.

Lucille [*enters; sits down on a stone beneath the* PRISONERS' *window*]. Camille! Camille! [CAMILLE *appears at the window.*] You're making me laugh, Camille, with that long stone coat and the iron mask on your face! Can't you bend down to me? Where are your arms?—I'll lure this tassel-gentle to me then: [*Sings.*]

> Two stars in Heaven are shining,
> Oh, brighter than the moon,
> One at my dear love's window,
> One at her chamber door.

Come, come, my love! Come quietly up the stairs, the house is sleeping. The moon has helped me wait for you all this time. But you can't come in the door, your costume's too unbearable. This is not a very funny joke, so please stop! You aren't moving either, why won't you say something? You're making me afraid.—Listen! People are saying you have to die, and making such long faces. Die! Their long faces make me laugh. Die! What kind of word is that? Tell me, Camille! Die! I must think about it. Oh, there, there it is—I must run after it; come, my love, help me catch it, come! Come!   *[She runs off.*

  Camille [*calls*]. Lucille! Lucille!

SCENE v—*The Conciergerie*

DANTON *at a window which looks into the adjoining room.*
CAMILLE, PHILIPPEAU, LACROIX, HÉRAULT-SÉCHELLES

DANTON. You're very quiet now, Fabre.

Fabre [*from within*]. Quiet as death.

Danton. Do you know what we'll be making soon?

Fabre [*from within*]. Well?

Danton. What you've spent your whole life making—*des vers.*

Camille [*to himself*]. There was madness behind those eyes. She's not the first to go mad—that's what the world makes of us. What can we do? Wash our hands! It's better that way.

Danton. I'm leaving everything in terrible confusion. Not one of them knows how to govern. It might still work, though, if I left my whores to Robespierre and my thighs to Couthon.

Lacroix. We'd be making Liberty a whore!

Danton. But that wouldn't have been much of a feat! Liberty and whores are the most cosmopolitan things under the sun. Liberty will prostitute herself honorably now in the marriage bed of the lawyer from Arras. But I think she'll play Clytemnestra on him. I give him less than six months before he follows me.

Camille [*to himself*]. Heaven help her to find some comfortable delusion. The universal delusion that we call

Reason is unbearably boring. The only way to be happy is imagine yourself Father, Son, and Holy Ghost all in one.

Lacroix. The asses will cry out: "Long live the Republic!" when we go by.

Danton. What does it matter? The flood of the Revolution can toss up our bodies wherever it likes, but they'll still be able to pick up our fossilized bones and smash in the heads of kings with them.

Hérault-Séchelles. Yes, if there happens to be a Samson around to find our jawbones.

Danton. They're all brothers of Cain.

Lacroix. And Robespierre's another Nero; look how friendly he was to Camille just two days before the arrest. Isn't that right, Camille?

Camille. I don't care—what does it matter? [*To himself.*] What a charming child she made of her madness! Why must I leave just now? We would have laughed with it, and rocked it, and kissed it.

Danton. If ever history opens our graves, despotism will suffocate from the stink of our dead bodies.

Hérault-Séchelles. We stank enough while we were alive.—But those are phrases for posterity, aren't they, Danton; they're none of our business.

Camille. From the face he's making you'd think he was turning it to stone for posterity to dig up as an antique.— Does it pay to put on false smiles, and rouge our cheeks, and speak with a fine accent? We ought to tear the masks off for once and look around as if in a room of mirrors, and everywhere see nothing but the ancient, innumerable, and imperishable head of a fool.—Nothing more, nothing less. The difference isn't so great, we're all rogues and angels, idiots and geniuses, in fact all of them in one: they all four find place enough in our bodies, they're not so large as people like to believe. Sleep, digest, procreate—it's what we all do; all the rest are only variations in different keys on the same theme. And still we have to go about on tiptoe and make faces, we still have to be embarrassed in front of one another! We've all stuffed ourselves sick at the same table and have a monumental bellyache; why cover our faces with our napkins? Cry and whimper as it happens to you! Just don't make such virtuous and clever and heroic and cheerful grimaces—after all, we know one another, so let's spare the trouble!

Hérault-Séchelles. Yes, we ought to sit down together and roar; what can be stupider than pressing our lips together when something hurts us. It was the Greeks and gods who roared, the Romans and Stoics sat there making heroic faces.

Danton. They were both Epicureans in their own way. Those Stoics gave themselves a comfortable feeling of self-respect. It's not at all bad to drape your toga around you and look about to see how long a shadow you're throwing. Why should we argue? What does it matter whether we cover our parts with laurel or roses or vine leaves or show the ugly thing in public for dogs to lick at!

Philippeau. No, my friends, we needn't get too high above the earth before all this confusion and glitter disappear and our eyes see only the few broad lines that God intended. There's an ear to which all this screaming and crying that we find so confusing is a stream of harmonies.

Danton. Except that we're the miserable musicians, our bodies the instruments. Do these ugly sounds that we bungle out of them exist only to float higher and higher and finally die out as softly as a voluptuous sigh in those heavenly ears?

Hérault-Séchelles. Are we suckling pigs that are whipped to death for the tables of princes, so that our flesh is more tasty?

Danton. Are we children roasted in the glowing Moloch-arms of the world and tickled with rays of light so that the gods can laugh?

Camille. Is the ether with its golden eyes nothing but a bowl of golden carp, set on the table of the blessèd gods, so that the blessèd gods can laugh eternally, and the fish die eternally, and the gods amuse themselves eternally with the play of colors of the death agony?

Danton. The world is chaos. Nothingness is the world-god yet to be born.

THE JAILER *enters.*

Jailer. Gentlemen, you may be on your way, your carriage is at the door.

Philippeau. Good night, my friends! Let us quietly pull
the great cover over us, under which all hearts beat their
last and all eyes fall shut. [*They embrace one another.*]

Hérault-Séchelles [*takes* CAMILLE's *arm*]. Cheer up,
Camille, it will be a nice night for it. Look there at the
clouds in the still evening sky—like a burnt-out Olympus,
with its dead, sinking forms of gods.   [*They go off.*

SCENE VI—A *room*

JULIE. People were running in the streets, but it's quiet
now.—I mustn't make him wait for even a moment. [*She
takes out a phial.*] Come, dearest priest, whose Amen
sends us to bed. [*She goes to the window.*] How lovely it
is to say good-bye like this; I have only to close the door
behind me. [*She drinks.*] I wish I could stand here forever.—The sun has gone down; earth's face looked so
sharp in its light, but now she's calm and solemn as a
dying woman. Twilight plays so beautifully on her brow
and cheeks.—She grows paler and paler, like a body sinking down into a sea of air. Will no one seize her by her
golden hair and pull her from the stream and bury her?—
I'll go quietly. I won't kiss her, for fear a breath or sigh
should wake her from her slumber.—Sleep, sleep! [*She
dies.*]

SCENE VII—*Place de la Révolution*

The carts are driven on and stop in front of the guillotine.
MEN *and* WOMEN *sing and dance the* Carmagnole. *The*
PRISONERS *begin singing the* Marseillaise.

A WOMAN WITH CHILDREN. Make room here! Give us
some room! My children are screaming, they're hungry.
I want to let them watch so they'll stop crying. Give us
some room here!

A *Woman.* Hey, Danton, you can pump away at the
worms now.

Another. You, Hérault, I'm going to have a wig made from your beautiful hair.

Hérault-Séchelles. Madame, I don't have enough hair to cover your denuded mound of Venus.

Camille. You damned bitches, you'll be crying soon enough for the mountains to fall on top of you!

A Woman. It's *you* the mountain's fallen on, or more likely you've fallen behind the mountain.

Danton [*to* CAMILLE]. Quiet, my boy! You've screamed yourself hoarse.

Camille [*gives the* CARTER *money*]. There, old Charon, your cart makes a good salver!—Gentlemen, permit me to serve myself up first. This is a classical supper we are invited to: we lie down to our places and scatter a bit of blood as a libation. Good-bye, Danton!

He ascends the scaffold, the PRISONERS *follow him one after the other.* DANTON *is the last to ascend.*

Lacroix [*to the* PEOPLE]. You killed *us* on the day when you lost your Reason; you will kill *them* on the day when you regain it.

Some Voices. Ha! We've heard that one before; try again! How boring!

Lacroix. The tyrants will break their necks over our graves!

Hérault-Séchelles [*to* DANTON]. He thinks his body's a hotbed of Liberty.

Philippeau [*on the scaffold*]. I forgive you; I hope that the hour of your death is no bitterer than mine.

Hérault-Séchelles. I knew it! He couldn't resist pulling out his shirt to show them down there he's got on clean linen!

Fabre. Farewell, Danton! I die twice over.

Danton. Good-bye, my friend! The guillotine is the best of all doctors.

Hérault-Séchelles [*tries to embrace* DANTON]. I'm sorry, Danton, I can't seem to manage a joke. The time has come. [*An* EXECUTIONER *pushes them apart.*]

Danton [*to the* EXECUTIONER]. Are you trying to be crueler than death? Do you think you can prevent our heads from kissing down there in the basket?

SCENE VIII—*A street*

LUCILLE. There must be something serious in it somewhere. I must think about that. I'm beginning to understand such things.—Dying—dying—!—But everything has
the right to live, everything, this little fly here, that bird.
Why not he? The stream of life would stop if even a drop
were spilt. The earth would suffer a wound from such a
blow.—Everything moves on, clocks tick, bells peal, people
run, water flows, and so on and on to—no, it mustn't
happen, no, I'll sit on the ground and scream, that all
things stop, in fear, that nothing goes any more, that
nothing moves. [*She sits on the ground, covers her eyes
and screams. After a moment she rises.*] It doesn't help,
nothing at all has changed: the houses, the streets, the
wind blowing, the clouds passing.—I suppose we must
bear it.

Several WOMEN *come down the street.*

First Woman. A handsome man, that Hérault!
Second Woman. On Constitution Day when I saw him
standing at the Arc de Triomphe, I said to myself, I said:
"Now there's one who'd look good up on the guillotine,"
really. Kind of a presentiment, you might say.
Third Woman. Yes, I think we need to see people in
all kinds of circumstances; I think it's a good thing that
dying's become so public.   [*They go past.*
  Lucille. O Camille! Where shall I look for you now?

SCENE IX—*Place de la Révolution*

Two EXECUTIONERS *busy with the guillotine.*

FIRST EXECUTIONER [*stands on the guillotine and sings*].
          And when I home do go
          By the moon's warm glow——
  Second Executioner. Hey! You almost done?
  First Executioner. In a minute, in a minute! [*Sings.*]
  My father stands at the door

Asking: "Where have you been with your whore?"
Here! Throw me the jacket!   [*They go off singing.*
Both Executioners [*sing*].
            And when I home did go
            By the moon's warm glow . . .
Lucille [*enters and sits on the steps of the guillotine*].
May I sit here in your lap, O silent Angel of Death?
Sings.]
            There is a Reaper, his name is Death,
            His power from Almighty God he hath.
My dear, sweet cradle that lulled my Camille to sleep,
you smothered him with your roses. And you, his death
bells, you sang him to his grave with your sweet voices.
Sings.]
            How many hundred thousands fall
            Beneath his sickle's pitiless call.

                    A PATROL *enters.*

A Citizen. Ho! Who's there?
Lucille [*reflective, and then as if making a decision,*
suddenly]. Long live the King!
Citizen. In the name of the Republic!

She is surrounded by the PATROL *and led away.*

LEONCE AND LENA

A Comedy

❧❦❧

Prologue
Alfieri: "E la Fama?"
Gozzi: "E la Fame?"

CHARACTERS

KING PETER, *of the kingdom of Popo*
PRINCE LEONCE, *his son, betrothed to Princess Lena*
PRINCESS LENA, *of the kingdom of Pipi*
VALERIO
THE GOVERNESS
THE PRIVATE TUTOR
THE MAJOR-DOMO
THE PRESIDENT OF THE COUNCIL OF STATE
THE COURT CHAPLAIN
THE DISTRICT MAGISTRATE
THE SCHOOLMASTER
ROSETTA
VALETS
SERVANTS
MEMBERS OF THE COUNCIL OF STATE
PEASANTS
SOLDIERS
MEMBERS OF THE COURT

LEONCE AND LENA

ACT ONE

> Oh! that I were a fool,
> I am ambitious for a motley coat.
> —*As You Like It*

SCENE I—*A garden*

LEONCE, *half resting on a bench, and the* PRIVATE TUTOR

LEONCE. Well, sir, what is it you want of me? Is it my vocation you wish to prepare me for? I'm so occupied with work at the moment that I scarcely know where to turn. Do you see this stone? My first duty is to spit down upon it three-hundred-and-sixty-five times in succession. Have you ever tried it? You must. It will accord you a most delicate source of diversion. And then . . . do you see this handful of sand? [*He takes up a handful of sand, tosses it into the air, and catches it again with the back of his hand.*] I throw it into the air. Shall we wager? How many grains of sand have I now on the back of my hand? An odd or an even number? What's that? You won't wager? You're not a heathen, are you? Do you believe in God? I generally wager with myself, in fact I can keep at it for days on end. However, if you happen to know where to find anyone who might occasionally take a fancy to laying wagers with me, I should be most indebted to you. And then . . . then I must ponder the possibilities of how I shall go about seeing the top of my head. Oh, for the man who shall see the top of his head for the first time! It's one of my ideals. I would need help, of course. And then . . . then an endless number of things of such sort. Am I an idler? Am I temporarily unoccupied? Yes, and isn't it sad . . .

Private Tutor. Very sad, Your Highness.

75

Leonce. That the clouds . . . the clouds have been drifting from west to east now for fully three weeks. It has made me terribly melancholy.

Private Tutor. A very well-founded melancholy.

Leonce. God! Why must you always agree with me! I'm certain you must have pressing business elsewhere, sir? I'm sorry for having detained you for so long. [*The* PRIVATE TUTOR *departs with a low bow.*] I congratulate you, sir, on the handsome parentheses of your legs when you bow. [*Alone,* LEONCE *stretches himself out upon the bench.*] The bees sit so languidly upon the flowers, and the sun's beams lie so lazily upon the ground. What dreadful indolence it brings with it. Indolence is the beginning of all evil. What people won't do out of mere boredom! They study out of boredom, pray out of boredom, they love, they marry and multiply out of boredom, and then at last they die out of boredom, and— what makes it so amusing—they do it with the most serious of countenances, without ever understanding why, and God knows what all else. These heroes, these geniuses, these simpletons, these saints, these sinners, these fathers of families, are, after all, nothing more than refined indolent idlers. Why must *I* be the one to know this? Why can't I be important to myself and dress this poor puppet in a frock coat and put an umbrella in his hand so that it will become very proper and very useful and very moral? The man who left me just now is a man whom I envy. I should have liked to thrash him out of envy. My God, to be able to be someone else! For only a moment. [VALERIO, *somewhat inebriated, enters.*] Look at the fool run! I wish I knew of only one thing under the sun that still could make me run like that.

Valerio [*stands close to* LEONCE, *places his finger at the side of his nose, and looks fixedly at him*]. Of course!

Leonce [*as above*]. Certainly!

Valerio. Do we understand each other?

Leonce. Completely.

Valerio. Good, then let's talk about something else. [*He lies down in the grass.*] In the meanwhile I'll lay myself down here on the lawn and let my nose blossom up through the leaves of grass, and then when the bees and the butterflies cradle themselves on it, as though it were a rose, I shall make allusions to romantic sentiments.

Leonce. Then you mustn't breathe so heavily, my good man, or the bees and butterflies that you've lured out of their flowers will die of starvation for not being able to light on that colossal prize.

Valerio. Oh, my lord, what a sense I have for Nature! The grass is so beautiful that one could wish he were a bull, to devour the grass, and then a man again, to digest the bull that devoured such beautiful grass.

Leonce. You poor unfortunate wretch, afflicted with ideals like the rest of us.

Valerio. What a pity! One can't jump off a church steeple without breaking his neck. One can't eat four pounds of cherries with their stones without having a bellyache. You know, my lord, I could sit in a corner from morning till night singing: "Ho, there's a fly, a fly on the wall! A fly on the wall! A fly on the wall!" and so on till the end of my life.

Leonce. Oh, keep quiet with your songs! They're enough to make a man a fool.

Valerio. At least he'd be *something.* A fool! What man will barter his foolhood against my reason? Ha! I'm an Alexander the Great! Look how the sun makes a golden crown of my hair, how my uniform sparkles! Lord General-issimo Grasshopper, let the troops advance! Lord Chancellor of the Exchequer, bring me some money! My dear Lady-in-Waiting Dragonfly, how is my precious spouse Madam Bean Pole getting on? And, my good Lord Doctor Spanish Fly, I am at a loss because of a prince who is heir to the throne.—And because of such exquisite fantasies as these one receives good soup, good meat, good bread, a good bed, and a gratuitous cutting of the hair— that is to say, in a madhouse—while I with my sound reason can, at best, do nothing more than take a position as one who promotes the advancement of blossoms on cherry trees, in order to . . . well? . . . to what?

Leonce. In order to turn the cherries red with embarrass-ment because of the holes in your trousers! But, my most excellent sir, what of your trade, your profession, your oc-cupation, your position, your skill?

Valerio [*with dignity*]. My lord, I have the grand occupation of being idle; I have an uncommon accomplishment in the art of doing nothing; I possess a colossal perseverance in slothfulness. You will find no calluses disgracing my hands, the earth has tasted no drop of the sweat of my brow, I am virginal in face of toil; and were it not too much bother, I should take pains to analyze for you at greater length these meritorious accomplishments.

Leonce [*with comic enthusiasm*]. Come to my bosom! Are you of those godlike beings who, with chaste brow, wander effortlessly through sweat and dust on the highway of life, and who, with lustrous feet and glowing body, tread, like the blessèd gods themselves, on to the Olympian Mount? Come to me! Come to me!

Valerio [*sings while leaving*]. "Ho, there's a fly, a fly on the wall! A fly on the wall! A fly on the wall!"

[*They go off arm in arm.*

SCENE II—A *room*

KING PETER *is being dressed by two of his* VALETS

KING PETER [*while being dressed*]. Man was made to think, and still I must think for my subjects; because they cannot think for themselves, cannot think for themselves. The substance of the matter is considered in the abstract, and *I* am that abstract. [*He runs about the room half-naked.*] Is that understood? To be considered in the abstract is to be considered in the abstract. Do you understand? And now my attributes come forward, my modifications, my affections and accidentals: where is my shirt, my trousers? Stop! Oh, shame! What do you mean leaving my free will here so exposed! What's happened to morality: where are my cuffs? The categories are in the most disgraceful confusion: two buttons too many have been buttoned; my snuffbox is in my right-hand pocket; in short, my entire system lies here in ruins. Ah-ha, what is the meaning of this button in my handkerchief? You, there, what is the meaning of this button, of what was I to remind myself?

First Valet. When Your Majesty deigned to deposit this button in his handkerchief, he intended to . . .

King Peter. Well?

First Valet. . . . to remind himself of something.

King Peter. A most intricate reply! Indeed! And now tell me what you meant by it.

First Valet. Your Majesty wanted to remind himself of something when he deigned to deposit this button in his handkerchief.

King Peter [*running back and forth*]. Of what? Of what? These people are confusing me, I am in utter confusion. I don't know what to do any more.

SERVANT *enters.*

Servant. Your Majesty, the Council of State is assembled.

King Peter [*happily*]. Of course, that's it, that's it! It was of my people that I wanted to remind myself! Come, gentlemen! Walk symmetrically now. Isn't it terribly warm? Do take your handkerchiefs and wipe your faces! I'm always so perplexed before a public speech.

All go off. Re-enter KING PETER, THE PRESIDENT, *and* THE COUNCIL OF STATE.

King Peter. My dear and faithful helpers, it is my intention that all men know by these presents, know by these presents . . . for, either my son will marry, or he will not marry . . . [*He places his finger at the side of his nose.*] . . . either, or . . . but do you understand me? There is no third alternative. Man must be made to think. [*He stands there for a moment musing.*] When I speak so loudly I scarcely know who it is who's speaking, myself or another, it frightens me. [*After long reflection.*] I am I. What do you think of that, my Lord President?

President [*with ceremonious slowness*]. Your Majesty, it may be so, and then again it may also not be so.

The Council of State [*in chorus*]. To be sure, it may be so, and then again it may also not be so.

King Peter [*with emotion*]. O my philosophers! Well now, what were we talking about? What was I about to say? My Lord President, why is it you have so short a memory on so festive an occasion? The Council is adjourned.

He leaves solemnly. The entire COUNCIL OF STATE *follows him.*

SCENE III—*A large, richly decorated hall with burning candles.*

LEONCE *with several* SERVANTS

LEONCE. Are all the shutters closed? Light the candles! I'll have no more to do with day! I want night, deep ambrosial night. Place the lamps under crystal shades and set them among the oleanders; I want them to seem like the eyes of young girls dreaming under leafy lashes. Push the roses closer, so that the wine may sparkle on the petals like drops of dew. Music! Where are the violins? Where is Rosetta? Away! All of you out!

The SERVANTS *go out.* LEONCE *stretches himself out on a sofa.* ROSETTA, *elegantly dressed, enters. There is music in the distance.*

Rosetta [*approaches fawningly*]. Leonce!
Leonce. Rosetta!
Rosetta. Leonce!
Leonce. Rosetta!
Rosetta. Your lips are languid. From kissing?
Leonce. From yawning!
Rosetta. Oh!
Leonce. Oh, Rosetta, I have the terrible task of . . .
Rosetta. Of what?
Leonce. . . . of doing nothing . . .
Rosetta. Except loving?
Leonce. Oh, that *is* work, isn't it!
Rosetta [*offended*]. Leonce!
Leonce. A vocation then!
Rosetta. Or indolence.
Leonce. Right as always. You are a shrewd young lady, and I place great confidence in your discernment.
Rosetta. Then you love me because you are bored?
Leonce. Not at all! I am bored because I love you. How-

ever, I am as fond of my boredom as I am of you. You are one and the same. *O dolce far niente!* I dream of your eyes as though they were wonderfully deep and hidden springs, your words of love make me drowsy as the murmur of waves. [*He embraces her.*] Come, dearest boredom, your kisses are voluptuous yawnings, and your gait like the pause between two vowels.

Rosetta. Then you love me, Leonce?

Leonce. Why not?

Rosetta. And forever?

Leonce. That's a long word: forever! Suppose I loved you for only five thousand years and seven months, would that be sufficient? Oh, I know it's far less than forever, but still and all it *is* a considerable time, and we can take our time loving one another.

Rosetta. Or time can take our loving from us.

Leonce. Or our loving take time. Dance for me, Rosetta, dance for me, so that time will pass with the measures of your dainty feet!

Rosetta. I'd rather my feet could take me out of time. [*She dances and sings.*]

And you, my weary feet, must dance, must dance
    In motley shoes.
How rather would you lie, deep, deep
    Beneath the yews.

And you, my burning cheeks, must glow, must glow
    With wild caresses.
How rather like white roses would you blow
    Beneath green tresses.

And you, sad eyes, must shimmer, you must shimmer
    With candlelight.
How rather would you lose yourselves in darkness
    Alone in night.

Leonce [*meanwhile lost in thought*]. Oh, a dying love is far more lovely than a flourishing one. I am a Roman: at our excellent banquets fishes of gold play their opalescent death games for our dessert. See how her cheeks grow pale, how soft her eyes grow tempered, how silently her undulating limbs rise and fall. Farewell, farewell, my love, I will love your lifeless body. [ROSETTA *approaches him again.*] Tears, Rosetta? A fine Epicurean trait, this sampling of sorrow. You must stand in the sun, so that these precious drops will crystallize; they should make splendid diamonds.

Rosetta. Diamonds, yes, for the way they cut my eyes! Oh, Leonce! [*Wanting to embrace him.*]

Leonce. Careful! My head! I have lain our love to rest within these temples. Look here into the windows of my eyes! Can you see how lovely the poor thing lies there in death? Can you see the two white roses on its breast? And therefore you must not touch me, lest one of its tiny arms be broken off, a lamentable thought. I must carry my head upright upon my shoulders now, like a woman carrying the coffin of a child.

Rosetta [jokingly]. You fool!

Leonce. Rosetta! [ROSETTA *grimaces.*] Thank God! [*He holds his eyes closed.*]

Rosetta [startled]. Leonce, look at me!

Leonce. Not for all the world!

Rosetta. Just once!

Leonce. Not even once! How can you say: "Just once," when that "Just once" will rewaken my dearest love? I'm glad to have buried it. I shall remember it as it was.

Rosetta [leaves sadly and slowly, singing as she goes].

> No one have I
> Afraid so all alone
> O Sorrow
> Come with me home . . .

Leonce [alone]. What a curious thing love is. One lies in bed for a whole year in a somnambulistic trance, and then wakens suddenly one beautiful morning, and runs his hand across his forehead and reflects . . . and reflects. My God, how many women we need to be able to sing the scale of love up and down again! One is scarcely enough to provide a single tone. Why must this haze over our earth be a prism to break down love's white ray of passion into a rainbow? [*He drinks.*] In what bottle is the wine hiding that's to make me drunk today? Or won't I ever get that far! I feel as if I were sitting under an air pump. The air's so rare and thin it makes me freeze, as if it wants me to skate around in nankeen trousers.—My

ords, my lords, tell me, do you know what Caligula and
Nero were? Tyrants out of boredom. Yes.—Come, Leonce,
et's have a monologue, I want to listen.—My life gapes
at me like a vast expanse of white paper which I'm to fill,
but I can't produce so much as a single letter. My head
is an empty ballroom: some wilted flowers and crumpled
ibbons on the floor, cracked violins in the corner, the last
lancers have taken off their masks and look at one another
with eyes tired as death. Twenty-four times a day I turn
myself inside out like a glove. Oh, I know myself, I know
what I'll be thinking and dreaming in a quarter of an hour
from now, in eight days, in a year from now. God, how
have I sinned that like a schoolboy Thou shouldst so often
scold me?—Bravo, Leonce! Bravo! [*He applauds.*] It does
me good to cheer myself that way. Ho, Leonce! Leonce!

Valerio [*speaking from under a table*]. Your Majesty
seems to be on the best of all possible ways to becoming
a veritable fool.

Leonce. Yes, all things considered, it appears much the
same to me.

Valerio. One moment, please, we must discuss this mat-
er in greater detail, and at once! But I have still just a
small piece of roast to eat up, which I pilfered out of the
kitchen, and a bit of wine from your table. I shall be
through in a moment.

Leonce. There he sits smacking his lips! He calls up all
sorts of idyllic sentiments in me. I could begin all over
again with the most simple of things. I could eat cheese,
drink beer, smoke tobacco. Get on with it, and don't grunt
so with that snout of yours! Don't click your teeth so
loud!

Valerio. Worthy Adonis, are you fearful for your thighs?
Don't let it trouble you, I'm neither a broombinder nor
a schoolmaster; I have no need to turn saplings into
switches.

Leonce. You owe me nothing.

Valerio. I wanted it to be the same for you, my lord.

Leonce. You mean to say you came for your thrashing?
Are you so concerned about your breeding?

Valerio. O Heaven, one arrives more easily at his be-
getting than at his breeding. It's sad how one circumstance

can leave another circumstance in the lurch! God, what I've labored through since my mother went into labor! How many blessings have I received that I can be thankful for the fact that I was conceived?

Leonce. As be*falls* your *conception*, nothing better could be*fall* it than to be *fallen* upon by *me.* Either improve your muddled *expression* or else feel the *impression* of my unpleasant *repression.*

Valerio. As my mother sailed around the Cape of Good Hope——

Leonce. And your father was shipwrecked on Cape Horn——

Valerio. True, he was a night watchman. Still, he didn't put the horn to his mouth as often as the fathers of highborn sons to their foreheads.

Leonce. You are possessed of most divine cheek. I sense a positive need of coming into closer contact with you. I have an unquenchable passion to thrash you.

Valerio. There's a striking resolution to a weighty argument!

Leonce [*approaching him threateningly*]. Or else *you* are a *defeated* resolution. For you'll be thrashed for your answer.

VALERIO *runs away;* LEONCE *stumbles and falls.*

Valerio. And *you* are an argument still in need of direction. He stumbles over his own legs, which actually are still a matter of argument. They are highly improbable calves and most problematic thighs.

THE COUNCIL OF STATE *enters.* LEONCE *remains seated on the floor.* VALERIO *is present.*

President. If Your Highness will pardon us . . .

Leonce. As though you were myself, my lord! As though you were myself! I shall pardon myself for the good nature I display in listening to you. Won't you be seated, my lords?—Look at the faces they make!—Please be seated on the floor, my lords, and you mustn't be embarrassed! You shall all arrive at this level in the end, though the only one ever to make a profit of it is the gravedigger.

President [*disconcertedly snapping his fingers*]. May it please Your Highness——

Leonce. But you mustn't snap your fingers so, unless you'd make a murderer of me!

President [*continues to snap his fingers even more loudly*]. Would Your Gracious Highness, in consideration——

Leonce. Good Heavens, my lord, either put your hands in your pockets or sit on them. He's utterly beside himself. Compose yourself, my lord!

Valerio. Never interrupt a child pissing, lest he develop a complex.

Leonce. I said to compose yourself! Think of your family, of the state! You'd be chancing an apoplectic fit if I were to withdraw from your presence.

President [*pulling a document from his pocket*]. With Your Highness' permission——

Leonce. What's this? You can read, too? Well, now . . .

President. His Royal Majesty, Your Father, the King of the Kingdom of Popo, would advise Your Royal Highness that tomorrow we have the honor of looking forward to the anticipated arrival of Your Highness' betrothed bride-to-be, Her Serene Highness, Princess Lena of the Kingdom of Pipi.

Leonce. If my bride-to-be awaits me, why then I shall concede to her will, and permit her to wait. I saw her yesterday evening in a dream: she had eyes so large that my Rosetta's ballet slippers had served as eyebrows for them; and on her cheeks I saw no lines of meditation, but a pair of drainage canals for when she laughs. I believe in dreams. Do you dream, too, at times, Lord President? Do you have presentiments, too?

Valerio. It stands to reason. It always happens on the night before the day on which a roast is burnt, a capon croaks, or His Royal Majesty has a bellyache.

Leonce. Apropos, was there something else you had to say? Please keep nothing from me.

President. On the day of the nuptials a High Will in the kingdom has determined to place into the hands of

Your Highness the manifestation of His most high design.

Leonce. You may tell the High Will that I shall do everything, except for that which I shall *not* do, which, however, shall not be very much, and that I shall do that "everything" as though it were twice as much as actually it is. My lords, you will pardon me if I do not accompany you, but just now I have a passion for sitting; but my pardon is so great that I can scarcely measure it with my legs. [*He spreads his legs wide on the floor.*] Lord President, would you take the measure, so that you can remind me of it at a later time. Valerio, you may bring my lord——

Valerio. Ring my lord? Do you mean I'm to box his ears? Or shall I lead him off on all fours as though he had a bell about his neck?

Leonce. You are nothing but a foul play on words. You have neither father nor mother, for the five vowels got together and begot you.

Valerio. And you, Prince, are a book without letters, a book filled with nothing but dashes. Come with me, my lords! There's something sad about the word "come." To have an income, one must steal; to come up in the world is quite unheard of, unless one hangs oneself; to come under protection is a state found only in burial, and a coming-out is what one suffers with one's wit when one is at a loss for words, as I am now, and like yourselves, even *before* you've opened your mouths. Having found your comeuppance, I shall now help you to find your outcome.

THE COUNCIL OF STATE *and* VALERIO *go out.*

Leonce [*alone*]. How common I must have made myself seem to the poor devils! But I suppose there is a certain profit to be gained from a certain degree of commonness. —Hm! Marriage! It's like drinking dry a draw well. O Shandy, old Shandy, who was it gave me your timepiece! [VALERIO *returns.*] Ah, Valerio! Have you heard?

Valerio. Why, yes, you're to be king. That's a jolly state of affairs. You can ride out all day and wear out your subjects' hats for all the pulling on and off you'll cause. And regular people can be cut to the measure of regular soldiers, so that everything will be more natural. Black frock coats and white cravats can be turned into civil servants. And when you die, all the polished buttons in your service will tarnish to blue, and the bell ropes will snap like threads of fancy from too much stress. Isn't that amusing?

Leonce. Valerio! Valerio! We must find something else to do! Help me!

Valerio. Ah, science, my lord, science! We shall become learnèd gentlemen! A priori? Or a posteriori?

Leonce. A priori . . . we'll have to learn that from my father; and a posteriori always starts off like the old fairy tales: Once upon a time . . .

Valerio. Well then, let's become heroes! [*He marches back and forth trumpeting and drumming.*] Trr-um, trr-um, trr-um-trr-um-trr-um! Da-da-da-da!

Leonce. But heroism is always expected to walk so far and always contracts hospital fever, and without lieutenants and recruits we'll never hold our own anywhere. You can pack up your Alexander and Napoleon romanticism!

Valerio. Then we'll become geniuses!

Leonce. All day long the Nightingale of Poetry sings its song above our heads, but the finest song always goes to waste until we pluck the Nightingale's plume and dip it in ink or colors.

Valerio. Suppose we become serviceable members of human society!

Leonce. I'd rather hand over my resignation as a human being.

Valerio. In that case why don't we just simply go to hell!

Leonce. Hell? Hell exists only as a contrast, so that we can the better conceive that something actually exists in Heaven. [*Jumping up.*] Ah! Valerio! Valerio! I *have* it! Don't you feel the southern breezes? Don't you feel the surging of the deep blue, glowing ether, the light flashing on the golden, sun-browned earth, on the hallowed sea, and the marble columns and statues? The great Pan is asleep, and the brazen figures, high above the deep murmur of the sea, dream, in shadows, of Vergil the Sorcerer, of the tarantella and the tambourine, of dark, extravagant

nights filled with masquerades and torches and guitar
We'll go as beggars, Valerio! We'll go as beggars! Valeri
we're going to Italy!

SCENE IV—A *garden*

PRINCESS LENA, *dressed as a bride, and the* GOVERNES

LENA. Yes, it has come at last. And here it is. Time seeme
so unimportant. It seemed to pass so lightly, and then on
day, suddenly, it rose up in front of me . . . and that wa
today. This garland circles my head . . . oh, and th
bells, the bells! [*She leans back and closes her eyes.*]
wanted the grass to cover me over, and the bees to buz
around above me. I've already dressed for the occasic
and have rosemary in my hair. I remember an old son
that goes:

> In the churchyard would I rest
> Like a child on mother's breast.

Governess. Poor child, how pale you are among all you
glittering precious stones!

Lena. O God, I *could* love someone, I *could!* We liv
so much apart, and feel for a hand to hold our own, unt
the time when the woman who tends us in death take
our hands apart and folds them across our breasts. Bu
why must they nail two hands together that have neve
sought one another? [*She takes a ring from her finger*
This ring stings me as though it were a viper.

Governess. But I've heard them say he's a regular Do
Carlos!

Lena. But . . . a man . . .

Governess. And?

Lena. . . . whom I do not love. [*She rises.*] Oh! Don'
you see how ashamed it makes me? Tomorrow all fragranc
and brightness will have been stripped from me. Must
be like the helpless pool that has to reflect on its silen
surface all that bends above it? These flowers open an
close their cups at will for the morning sun or against th
evening wind. Is the daughter of a king any less than
flower?

Governess [*weeping*]. Poor, poor lamb, I know, I know, you *are* just an innocent sacrifice!

Lena. Yes, and the priest already raising the knife. My God, my God, is it true then that we must redeem ourselves with our own suffering? Is it true then that the world is a crucified Saviour, the sun its crown of thorns, and the stars the nails and spears in its feet and side?

Governess. My child, my child! I can't bear to see you like this. This can't go on this way, it will kill you.— Perhaps . . . but who knows! There's a thought that just came to me. We shall see. Come!   [*She leads* LENA *away.*]

ACT TWO

How a voice was ringing, ringing
          Out within me.
In a moment quite extinguishing
          My memory.

—ADALBERT VON CHAMISSO

SCENE I—*An open field. An inn in the background*

LEONCE *and* VALERIO, *carrying a pack, enter.*

VALERIO [*panting*]. On my honor, Prince, this world's just too large a place.

Leonce. Certainly not! Certainly not! I haven't even the courage to stretch out my arms as if I were in a narrow room of mirrors. I'm afraid of colliding with them every time I move, till finally the lovely forms I see mirrored in them lie shattered at my feet, and I find myself standing in front of a bare naked wall.

Valerio. I'm lost.

Leonce. The only one to pity is the one who finds you.

Valerio. My next move will be to stand in my shadow's shadow.

Leonce. Yes, the sun will soon evaporate you. Do you see those lovely clouds up there? At least a quarter of them must be you. See how comfortably they look down at your grosser material stuff.

Valerio. Those clouds couldn't hurt *your* head any if they were let precipitate on it drop by drop. What a priceless idea!—We've already traveled through a dozen principalities, through half a dozen grand duchies, and through several royal kingdoms, and all this in the rash haste of half a day. And why? Because you are expected to become king and marry a beautiful princess! And still you insist on continuing as you are. I can't understand your resignation. I can't understand why you didn't simply take arsenic, clamber up the balustrade of a church steeple, and fire a shot into your skull so as to avoid your fate.

Leonce. It's the ideal, Valerio, the ideal! I have in my mind the ideal woman, and I must find her. She is infinitely beautiful and infinitely unintellectual. Her beauty is as helpless and pathetic as a newborn child. What an exquisite contrast: those divinely vacuous eyes, this excellently simple mouth, the straight-nosed Grecian profile: this intellectual death in this unintellectual body.

Valerio. Damnation! Here we are at another border already. This country's like an onion: nothing but layer after layer; or like a series of boxes inside one another: in the biggest there are only smaller boxes, and in the smallest, nothing. [*He tosses his pack to the ground.*] Is this pack to be my gravestone? Excuse me, Prince, if I become philosophical . . . but here I am, symbol of the human condition: all day long, with sore feet, through frost and sunburn, I lug this pack about, and only because when evening comes I want to be able to put on a clean shirt. But when evening finally comes, my brow is furrowed, my cheeks are hollow, my eyes grown dim, and I scarcely have time enough to pull on my clean shirt to serve as my shroud. Wouldn't it have been better if I had simply lifted my pack off this stick and sold it at the first good inn I came to, and then have got drunk with the money and slept in the shade until evening, never to have sweated or run corns on my feet? And now, Prince, to the application: now, out of nothing but sheer false modesty, we want to cover up the inner man, we want to dress ourselves in coat and trousers. [*They both go to the inn.*]

Ho, there, old pack, get a good noseful of that smell: wine and juicy roasts! God, how these pants of mine would like to root in the ground and blossom out like fruit trees. And long, heavy clusters of grapes reach down for my mouth, and new wine ferment under the wine press.

They go off. PRINCESS LENA *and* THE GOVERNESS *enter.*

Governess. I think the day must be bewitched; the sun won't set, and it seems so endlessly long since we fled.

Lena. Not really. The flowers I gathered as we passed out through the garden are scarcely wilted.

Governess. And besides that, where will we stay? We haven't found a single place yet. I haven't seen a cloister, or a hermitage, or even a shepherd.

Lena. We dreamed of it all so differently from our books, behind the walls of our garden, walking among the myrtle and the oleander.

Governess. Oh, the world is a detestable place! We might just as well give up all hope of running across a wandering prince.

Lena. Oh, but the world's so large and so beautiful, so infinitely large! I'd like to go on like this forever, night and day. There's not a thing moving. Look there, the red radiance of blossoms playing across the meadow, and the faraway mountains resting upon the earth like slumbering clouds.

Governess. Sweet Jesus, what will they say! And still she's so tender, so womanly! It's as good as an abjuration. It's like the flight of Saint Ottilia herself. But we must find a shelter: it will soon be evening!

Lena. Yes, the flowers close their tiny leaves in sleep, and the sun's rays cradle themselves in the long grass like weary dragonflies.

SCENE II—*The inn on a high hill beside a river. A view in the distance. A garden in front of the inn*

VALERIO *and* LEONCE

VALERIO. Well, my lord, don't your trousers deliver you a delicious beverage? Don't your boots wend their way down your throat with the greatest of ease?

Leonce. Do you see those trees, the hedgerows, the

flowers? They all have their history, their lovely, secret
history. Do you see the friendly faces of the old men sitting under the grape arbor, there in front of the inn?
How they sit there holding one another's hands, afraid
to think of how old they are and how young the world
still is. Oh, Valerio, and here I am so young and the world
so old! Sometimes I'm so afraid, that I could sit in a
corner and weep hot tears in sympathy with myself.

Valerio [*giving a glass*]. Take this bell, this diving bell,
and sink yourself into a sea of wine until you see shining
bubbles singing above your head. Then watch the elves
hover over the wine's bouquet, golden-sandaled and sound-
ing their cymbals.

Leonce [*jumping up*]. Come, Valerio, we must find
something to do! We'll devote ourselves to deep thoughts;
we'll investigate how it is that a stool stands on three legs
instead of two. We'll dissect ants, count the filaments of
flowers! I'll even transform it into a princely amusement.
I'll find a child's rattle which won't fall from my hands
until I begin to lecture the snowflakes and tug at the
covers. I still have a good store of enthusiasm to exhaust;
but then when I have everything hot and cooked to a
turn, I'll need an endless amount of time to find a spoon
with which to eat the dish, and that's why I've given up
the whole idea.

Valerio. *Ergo bibamus!* This bottle is no mistress, no
concept; it'll cause you neither the pains of birth nor
boredom; never unfaithful, it'll stay with you from the
first drop to the last. All you do is break the seal and all
the dreams dozing inside come surging out.

Leonce. My God! A straw! A straw! Half a life of
prayer for a straw to ride upon like a splendid stallion,
until I end lying in the hay!—What a sinister evening
this is! It's all so quiet down there, and up here the
clouds do nothing but billow and surge, and the sunlight
comes and goes. Look at those strange figures down there,
rushing along! The long shadow with horribly thin legs
and the wings of a bat! And all so quickly, so chaotically,
with nothing else moving, neither a leaf nor a blade of
grass. The earth draws itself together like a frightened
child, as the ghosts stride across its cradle.

Valerio. I don't know what it is you want; I'm very comfortable. The sun looks to me like a sign hanging outside an inn, and the fiery clouds above it like the inscription: INN OF THE GOLDEN SUN. The earth and water down below are like a table on which wine has been spilled, and we lie upon it like playing cards which God and the devil play with out of boredom; you're the king and I'm the joker, and the only thing still missing is a lady, a lovely lady, with a gingerbread heart on her breast and a gigantic tulip into which she sentimentally sinks her pointed nose . . . [THE GOVERNESS *and* PRINCESS LENA *enter.*] . . . and, by God, here she is! It isn't quite a tulip she has, but a pinch of snuff, nor is it exactly a nose, but a proboscis. [*To* THE GOVERNESS.] Why are you walking so fast, my good woman, so that we may see all the way up what were once your calves to your respectable garters?

Governess [*severely irritated, she stops short*]. And why, my good man, must you open your muzzle so wide that it seems a crevasse has opened in the landscape?

Valerio. So that you, my good woman, will not bloody your nose by colliding with the horizon. A nose such as yours is like unto the Tower of Lebanon on the road toward Damascus.

Lena [*to* THE GOVERNESS]. My dear, why is it such a long way?

Leonce [*daydreaming*]. Oh, all ways are long. The peck of the deathwatch beetle in our breasts is slow, and every drop of blood is lost, and our life is a lingering fever. For feet that are weary all ways are long . . .

Lena [*listening to him with uneasy contemplation*]. And for eyes that are weary every shaft of light is too harsh, and for lips that are weary every breath is too difficult, [*smiling*] and for ears that are weary every word is one too many.

She goes into the inn with THE GOVERNESS.

Leonce. O Valerio! Couldn't I just as well have said: "Would not this, sir, and a forest of feathers—if the rest of my fortunes turn Turk with me—with two Provincial roses on my razed shoes, get me a fellowship in a cry of players, sir?" It seems to me I said it with such melancholy. Thank God I'm beginning to come down with this melancholy! The air is no longer so clear and cold, the Heavens have encircled me like glowing embers, and heavy drops of dew are falling about me.—Oh, the sound of her voice: "Why is it such a long way?" The world has many voices, they say, and they all speak of different things, but I understood her. She descends upon me like the Spirit which hovered upon the waters before Light was. The depths of my heart seethed, and there was such growth inside me as I heard her voice tremble in space! "Why is it such a long way?"   [He goes out.

Valerio. No, it's not a very long way to the madhouse; it's not hard to find, I know all the highways and byways. He's already on his way there. I can see him now, on a broad avenue, on an ice-cold winter day, his hat under his arm, as he stands in the long shadows of bare trees, fanning himself with his handkerchief.—He's a fool!

He follows LEONCE *off.*

SCENE III—*A room*

LENA *and* THE GOVERNESS

GOVERNESS. The nerve of those men!

Lena. He seemed so old, and still he's so very young. His face was as warm as spring, and his heart as cold as winter. That's a sad thing. A weary body can always find a place to rest, but what of a weary mind? I've just had a terrible thought: I believe there are people who are unhappy, and incurably so, simply because they exist. [*She rises.*]

Governess. Where are you off to, my child?

Lena. To the garden.

Governess. But . . .

Lena. But what, my sweet? You know as well as I that I should have been planted in a flowerpot when I was a child. I need the dew and the night air as much as the flowers do. Can you hear the sounds the night makes? How the crickets sing the day to sleep and the night

violets lull it with their fragrance! How can I stay indoors!
It's as if the walls were collapsing on me!

SCENE IV—*The garden. Night. Moonlight*

LENA *is seen sitting on the grass.* VALERIO *speaks off stage.*

VALERIO [*at a distance*]. Nature's a lovely thing, but how
much lovelier it would be without these gnats, and if the
beds in the inn were a little cleaner, and if the deathwatch beetles didn't peck so inside the walls. Inside, the
snores of sleeping humanity and outside the croak of
waking frogs; inside, the whirring of domestic crickets
and outside the whirring of field crickets. O blessèd turf,
what a grass-eating decision! [*He lies down on the grass.*]

Leonce [*entering*]. O blessèd night, soft as the first that
settled on Paradise! [*He notices* LENA *and approaches her
quietly.*]

Lena [*to herself*]. A bird singing in its dreams.—How
softly the night sleeps, its cheek so pale, its breathing so
silent. The moon is like a slumbering child, its golden
curls tumbled down in sleep over its precious forehead.
Its sleep is death. Like a lifeless angel lying on a dark
cushion, and the stars, like candles, burning round about
him! How sad it is, to be dead and so alone.

Leonce. Rise up then in your moon-white dress and
wander through the night behind its lifeless form and sing
it a song of death!

Lena. Who's there?

Leonce. A dream.

Lena. Dreams, they say, are blest.

Leonce. Then dream yourself blest and let me be your
blessèd dream.

Lena. Death is the most blessèd dream.

Leonce. Then let me be your Angel of Death! Let my
lips, like his wings, light upon your eyes. [*He kisses her.*]
Lovely, lifeless form, you rest so sweetly upon the pall of
night that Nature, grown tired of living, is enamored of
death.

Lena. Please, you mustn't! [*She jumps up and hurries
off.*]

Leonce. My God! My God! All my being existed in

that single moment! I wish I could die! What more can
there be? How fresh and clean all things seem to me
now as they wrest their way from chaos! The earth is a
golden bowl sparkling with light that overflows its sides,
and the stars are bubbles rising out of it. This single drop
of blessèdness has turned me into a priceless vessel. Let me
cast it away! [*He tries to throw himself into the river.*]

Valerio [*jumps up and catches him*]. Ho there, Your
Highness!

Leonce. Let me go!

Valerio. I'll let you go as soon as you give over and
promise to let the river be.

Leonce. You fool!

Valerio. Hasn't Your Highness been cured yet of his
lieutenant's romanticism: breaking the glass when he's
drunk to his sweetheart's health?

Leonce. You know, I almost think you're right.

Valerio. Take it easy! You may not sleep *under* the
turf tonight, but you'll at least sleep *on* it. It's no less
suicidal sleeping in one of those beds than it is jumping
into the river. You'd feel like a corpse stretched out on
that hay in there, until the fleas started to bite at you
as if you were alive.

Leonce. It's all the same to me. [*He lies down on the
grass.*] You fool, you've saved me from the most beautiful
suicide I'll ever find! I'll never live through another moment as well suited to it, and such excellent weather, too.
I'm not in the mood now. This fool with his yellow coat
and sky-blue pants ruined it all.—May Heaven give me
a good, sound, heavy sleep!

Valerio. Amen!—And *I* saved a human life. May my
good conscience keep my body warm.

Leonce. A lot of good it'll do you, Valerio!

ACT THREE

SCENE I—A *garden*

LEONCE *and* VALERIO

VALERIO. Marriage? Well, when did Your Highness give
in so easily?

Leonce. Did you know, Valerio, that even the most insignificant of human beings is so important that a lifetime is far too short to give him the love he deserves? And as far as that man is concerned who thinks that there is nothing so beautiful or so sacred but that he can make it even *more* beautiful or *more* sacred, I can ignore him. There's a certain satisfaction in this precious arrogance, I suppose. Why should I begrudge it him?

Valerio. Very humane, and very much the lover of beasts! But does she know who you are?

Leonce. She knows only that she loves me.

Valerio. And does Your Highness know who *she* is?

Leonce. You simple fool! Why not ask the pinks and dewdrops for their names!

Valerio. That is to say, at least she's *something*, unless that's a bit too tactless and savors of a police warrant.— But how are we going to arrange this?—Hm! Your Highness, will you appoint me your Minister of State, if today, in the midst of the wedding celebration, and in front of your father, I can manage to have you joined to this inexplicable being without a name? Do I have your word?

Leonce. You have my word!

Valerio. May this poor devil Valerio bid adieu to His Excellency the Lord Minister of State, Valerio of Valeriental.—"What does this fellow want? I don't recognize him. Away with you, rascal!"

He runs off; LEONCE *follows him.*

SCENE II—*An open plaza in front of the castle of* KING PETER

THE DISTRICT MAGISTRATE, THE SCHOOLMASTER, *and* PEASANTS *in their Sunday best, holding branches of fir trees.*

DISTRICT MAGISTRATE. I say there, Schoolmaster, how are your people getting on?

Schoolmaster. They're getting on so well with their maladies that for a long time now they've even been getting on with one another. If it weren't for the good spirits they pour down their throats they'd never get on so well in this heat. Courage, people! Here, here! You must hold your fir-tree boughs directly in front of you. Then any passer-by will think it a fir-tree forest, and your noses strawberries, and your three-cornered hats the antlers of wild game, and your buckskin pants the moonlight in the forest. And remember, when you walk, each one directly behind the one in front of him, so that it looks as if you were nurtured in a quadrant.

District Magistrate. And you, Schoolmaster, are standing on the verge of sobriety.

Schoolmaster. Understood! I can hardly stand *because* of sobriety.

District Magistrate. Pay attention now, people; it stands written here in the program: "The assembled subjects shall, of their own free will, be cleanly clothed, well-fed, and with contented countenances display themselves along the main thoroughfare." So don't put us to shame!

Schoolmaster. Stand ready now! Don't scratch behind your ears and don't blow your noses as long as the Royal Procession is passing; and remember, be moved by the proper emotions or we may have to employ more moving means. And finally, you will be pleased to note the consideration being shown you: you have been so placed that the scent from the kitchen cannot fail to pass you by, so that none of you will die without the benefit of at least having smelled a roast. Do you still remember your lessons? Hm! *Vi!*

The Peasants. Vi!
Schoolmaster. Vat!
The Peasants. Vat!
Schoolmaster. Vivat!
The Peasants. Vivat!

Schoolmaster. There, my Lord District Magistrate! You can see how intelligence is on the rise in our fair community! Just think! Latin! This evening, however, we are holding a transparency ball with the help of the holes in our trousers and jackets, and we shall strike cockades onto our heads with our fists.

SCENE III—A *great hall*

Finely dressed LADIES *and* GENTLEMEN, *carefully grouped.*
THE MAJOR-DOMO, *with several* SERVANTS, *in the fore-
ground.*

MAJOR-DOMO. What a terrible state of affairs! Everything
will be ruined! The roasts are shriveling up. Congratula-
tions are growing stale. The gentlemen's stand-up collars
are wilting like melancholy pigs' ears. The peasants' nails
and beards are growing long again. The soldiers' newly
curled hair is coming uncurled. And of the twelve virgins
in attendance, there isn't one who wouldn't prefer the
horizontal approach as the proper one.

First Servant. In their white dresses they look like white
exhausted silk rabbits, and the court poet is grunting his
way around them like a distressed guinea pig. The officers,
for all their bearing, and the ladies of the court, are like
salt statues with all their perspiring.

Second Servant. At least they're making themselves
comfortable; no hidden shoulders *here*. And even if they're
not openhearted, at least they're open down *to* the heart.

Major-domo. Yes, excellent relief maps of the Turkish
Empire: especially the Dardanelles and the Sea of Mar-
mara. Away with you rascals! His Majesty is coming!

KING PETER *and the* COUNCIL OF STATE *enter.*

King Peter. So now the Princess has disappeared, too.
Has no one found a trace yet of our beloved Crown Prince?
Are my orders being carried out? Are the borders being
watched?

Major-domo. Yes, Your Majesty. The view from this
hall permits us the strictest surveillance. [*To* THE FIRST
SERVANT.] What have you seen?

First Servant. A dog that ran through the kingdom
looking for its master.

Major-domo [*to the other*]. And you?

Second Servant. There's someone strolling along the
north border, but it's not the Prince, I'd recognize him.

Major-domo. And you?

Third Servant. If you'll pardon me, nothing.

Major-domo. That's very little. And you?

Fourth Servant. Nothing either.

Major-domo. That's scarcely more than the other.

King Peter. But, my dear Council of State, was it not our resolve that My Royal Majesty would rejoice on this day and that the marriage would be celebrated on it? Was that not our steadfast decision?

President. Yes, Your Majesty, that is the way it stands in the minutes and was made a matter of record.

King Peter. And should I not be guilty of compromise if I failed to execute my resolve?

President. If it were possible for Your Majesty to do otherwise, *then* we should have a case of compromise, but . . .

King Peter. Have I given My Royal Word?—Yes: I shall set my resolve to work at once: I shall rejoice. [*He rubs his hands together.*] Oh, I am extraordinarily jubilant!

President. We will all of us share in Your Majesty's sentiments so far as is possible and proper for subjects.

King Peter. Oh, I am so happy that I cannot contain myself! I shall have red jackets made for my valets, I shall promote some cadets to lieutenant, I shall permit my subjects . . . but, but what of the marriage? Doesn't the other half of the resolve read that the marriage is to be celebrated?

President. Yes, Your Majesty.

King Peter. Yes; but if neither the Prince *nor* the Princess arrives . . .

President. Yes, if neither the Prince *nor* the Princess arrives, then . . . then . . .

King Peter. Then? Then?

President. Then they simply cannot be married.

King Peter. One moment! Is this conclusion logically founded? If . . . then . . . Very good! But My Royal Word!

President. Your Majesty may take consolation in the examples of other Majesties! A Royal Word is something which . . . which . . . which is . . . nothing whatever.

King Peter [*to* THE SERVANTS]. Do you see anything yet?

Servants. Nothing, Your Majesty, nothing at all.

King Peter. And I had resolved so to rejoice! Precisely at the stroke of twelve I wanted to begin and to rejoice for fully twelve hours . . . I'm becoming so melancholy.

President. All subjects will be called upon to share in the sentiments of Your Majesty.

Major-domo. For those subjects, however, without handkerchiefs, weeping will, in the interests of decency, be prohibited.

First Servant. Wait! What's that? It looks like a protrusion, like a nose, the rest of it isn't across the boundary yet; and then there's another man, and then two other persons of opposite sexes.

Major-domo. What's their direction?

First Servant. They're coming closer. They're approaching the castle. They've arrived!

VALERIO, LEONCE, THE GOVERNESS *and* LENA *enter, masked.*

King Peter. Who may you be?

Valerio. How should I know? [*He removes a series of masks from his face, one after another.*] Am I this one? Or this? Or this? You know, it frightens me when I think that I might peel myself away to nothing, one layer after another.

King Peter [*confused*]. But . . . but you *must* be *something,* mustn't you?

Valerio. Well, if Your Majesty insists! But in that case, my lords, you must turn the mirrors around and hide your polished buttons a bit, and you mustn't look at me so that I can see myself mirrored in your eyes, or I may *never* know who I am.

King Peter. He's making me terribly confused, driving me to desperation! I'm utterly perplexed!

Valerio. However, what I really wanted to announce to this high and honorable assembly was that the two world-famous automatons had arrived, and that I am perhaps the third and most curious of them both, if only I knew who I am, a topic about which we are not permitted to think, since I haven't the faintest idea what I'm talking about, in fact I don't even know that I *don't* know, so that it's highly probable that I'm merely being *let* talk, because after all it's only some tubes and hot air that's saying this. [*In a raspy voice.*] Here, ladies and gentlemen, you see two individuals of either sex, a man and a woman, a gentleman and a lady! They are nothing more than artifice and mechanical ingenuity, pasteboard and watch springs! Each is equipped with a delicate, delicate ruby spring under the nail of the small toe of the right foot. Press this lever ever so gently and the mechanism will be set in motion for fully fifty years. These individuals are so consummately constructed that they cannot be distinguished from other human beings, unless one knows that they are merely pasteboard; they might even be accepted as members of human society. They are very well born, because they speak High German; they are very moral, because they rise punctually at the stroke of a bell, because they eat punctually at the stroke of midday, and because they retire punctually at the stroke of another bell; and then, too, they have a good digestion, which attests to a clear conscience. They possess a delicately ethical sense of feelings, because the lady never has leave to speak of the concept of women's drawers, and it is utterly impossible for the gentleman to precede the lady, in either climbing or descending a flight of stairs, by so much as a single step. They are very well educated, because the lady sings all the new operas and the gentleman wears cuffs. Pay attention now, ladies and gentlemen, for they are now in an interesting stage of their development: the mechanism of love is beginning to set itself in motion. The gentleman has already given the lady her scarf a number of times, and several times now the lady has rolled her eyes and turned them toward heaven. Both of them have whispered together a number of times: about faith, and love, and hope! They already seem very much in accord, all that's lacking now is that paltry word: Amen.

King Peter [*placing a finger beside his nose*]. In effigy? In effigy? My Lord President, when one has a person hanged in effigy, isn't it just as good as hanging him in person?

President. Oh, much better, Your Majesty, much better,

because he suffers no injury that way, and still he has
been hanged.

King Peter. I *have* it! We will celebrate the marriage
in effigy! [*Indicating* LEONCE *and* LENA.] This is the
Princess, and this is the Prince. [*Delightedly.*] Oh, I shall
carry through my resolve and then rejoice! Let the bells
ring out! Prepare yourself for our felicitations! Please,
hurry, my Lord Court Chaplain!

THE COURT CHAPLAIN *enters, clears his throat, looks*
toward heaven a number of times.

Valerio. Begin! Blast your cursèd faces, let's start! Now
then!

Court Chaplain [*in utter confusion*]. If we . . . well
. . . suppose then . . .

Valerio. Because . . .

Court Chaplain. Because . . .

Valerio. . . . in the beginning before the world
was . . .

Court Chaplain. That is . . .

Valerio. . . . the Lord God found that He was
bored . . .

King Peter. Make it short, my good man, make it short.

Court Chaplain [*composing himself*]. If it please Your
Highness, Prince Leonce of the Kingdom of Popo, and
if it please Your Highness, Princess Lena of the Kingdom
of Pipi, and if it please Your Highnesses reciprocally,
mutually to desire one another, then indicate the same
with a loud and clear: Yea.

Leonce and Lena. Yea!

Court Chaplain. And to that I say: Amen.

Valerio. Well done, short and to the point. And so
the Lord God created Man and Woman, and all the
beasts of Paradise stood round about them.

LEONCE *removes his mask.*

All. The Prince!

King Peter. The Prince! My son! I'm lost, I've been
deceived! I declare everything null and void!

Governess [*removes* LENA's *mask, triumphantly*]. The
Princess!

Leonce. Lena?

Lena. Leonce?

Leonce. And I thought we were escaping into Paradise.

Lena. I have been deceived!

Leonce. I have been deceived!

Lena. It was all an accident, then?

Leonce. It was all Providence!

Valerio. I'm sorry, but I can't help laughing! I can't help laughing! It seems that all things fall out: Your Highnesses have fallen to one another's lot; I hope you will let this fall-out of fortune fall to your good fortune, and fall for one another fully.

Governess. O that my eyes should see what they have longed for all these years! A wandering prince! Now I can die in peace!

King Peter. My dear children, my emotions are so moved that I scarcely know what to do with them. I am the most fortunate of men! I herewith, however, solemnly place into your hands, my son, my reign; and I shall devote myself at once to uninterrupted thought. But, my son, you must leave me these wise philosophers [*he signifies his* COUNCIL OF STATE], so that they may support me in my endeavors. Come, my lords, we must give ourselves to thought, uninterrupted thought! This individual plunged me into an abyss of confusion just a moment ago, I must look into rescuing myself from it.

[*He leaves with* THE COUNCIL OF STATE.]

Leonce [*to those present*]. My subjects! My wife and I regret terribly that you have been put to so long service for us today. Your station is so wretched that we have no desire to put your constancy to the test any longer. You may go to your homes now, but you must forget neither how to speak, nor your sermons, nor your verses, for tomorrow, in all peace and kindliness, we will begin the joke all over again. Good-bye!

All leave, LEONCE, LENA, VALERIO, *and* THE GOVERNESS *excepted.*

Leonce. And so, Lena, you see how our pockets are stuffed with puppets and playthings. What shall we do with them? Shall we make mustaches for them and hang

broadswords about their waists? Or shall we dress them
in frock coats and let them practice infusorial politics and
diplomacy, and sit here watching them through our microscopes? Or would you prefer a barrel-organ on which
milk-white esthetic shrews flit about? Shall we build a
theatre? [LENA *leans against him, shakes her head.*] Oh,
but I know what it is you really want: we shall have all
the clocks in the kingdom destroyed, forbid all calendars,
and count off hours and months with the chronometer of
the flowers, according to times of planting and times of
harvest. And then we shall surround our tiny kingdom
with burning glasses so that winter no longer exists, and
in summer we shall rise up through a process of distillation
as high as Ischia and Capri, and all year long live amidst
roses and violets, surrounded with orange and laurel
boughs.

Valerio. And I'll be the Minister of State, and I'll issue
a decree which reads: that anyone who works calluses on
his hands will be placed in custody of a guardian; that
anyone who works himself sick will be criminally prosecuted; that every man who prides himself on eating bread
earned in the sweat of his brow will be declared insane
and a hazard to human society. And then we shall lie in
the shade and ask the Lord God for macaroni, melons,
and figs, for voices soft as music, for bodies fine as classical heroes, and for a commodious religion!

WOYZECK

CHARACTERS

WOYZECK
MARIE
CAPTAIN
DOCTOR
DRUM MAJOR
SERGEANT
ANDRES
MARGRET
PROPRIETOR OF THE BOOTH
CHARLATAN
OLD MAN WITH BARREL-ORGAN
JEW
INNKEEPER
APPRENTICES
KATHY
KARL THE TOWN IDIOT
GRANDMOTHER
POLICEMAN
SOLDIERS, STUDENTS, YOUNG MEN *and* GIRLS, CHILDREN, JUDGE,
    COURT CLERK, PEOPLE

WOYZECK

SCENE I—At the CAPTAIN'S

THE CAPTAIN *in a chair.* WOYZECK *shaving him.*

CAPTAIN. Not so fast, Woyzeck, not so fast! One thing at a time! You're making me dizzy. What am I to do with the ten extra minutes that you'll finish early today? Just think, Woyzeck: you still have thirty beautiful years to live! Thirty years! That makes three hundred and sixty months! And days! Hours! Minutes! What do you think you'll do with all that horrible stretch of time? Have you ever thought about it, Woyzeck?

Woyzeck. Yes, sir, Captain.

Captain. It frightens me when I think about the world . . . when I think about eternity. Busyness, Woyzeck, busyness! There's the eternal: that's eternal, that is eternal. That you can understand. But then again it's not eternal. It's only a moment. A mere moment. Woyzeck, it makes me shudder when I think that the earth turns itself about in a single day! What a waste of time! Where will it all end? Woyzeck, I can't even look at a mill wheel any more without becoming melancholy.

Woyzeck. Yes, sir, Captain.

Captain. Woyzeck, you always seem so exasperated! A good man isn't like that. A good man with a good conscience, that is. Well, say something, Woyzeck! What's the weather like today?

Woyzeck. Bad, Captain, sir, bad: wind!

Captain. I feel it already. Sounds like a real storm out there. A wind like that has the same effect on me as a mouse. [*Cunningly.*] I think it must be something out of the north-south.

Woyzeck. Yes, sir, Captain.

Captain. Ha! Ha! Ha! North-south! Ha! Ha! Ha! Oh, he's a stupid one! Horribly stupid! [*Moved.*] Woyzeck,

109

you're a good man, but [*With dignity.*] Woyzeck, you
have no morality! Morality, that's when you have morals,
you understand. It's a good word. You have a child without the blessings of the Church, just like our Right
Reverend Garrison Chaplain says: "Without the blessings
of the Church." It's not *my* phrase.

Woyzeck. Captain, sir, the good Lord's not going to
look at a poor worm just because they said Amen over it
before they went at it. The Lord said: "Suffer little
children to come unto me."

Captain. What's that you said? What kind of strange
answer's that? You're confusing me with your answers!

Woyzeck. It's us poor people that . . . You see, Captain, sir . . . Money, money! Whoever hasn't got money
. . . Well, who's got morals when he's bringing something like me into the world? We're flesh and blood, too.
Our kind is miserable only once: in this world and in the
next. I think if we ever got to Heaven we'd have to help
with the thunder.

Captain. Woyzeck, you have no virtue! You're not a
virtuous human being! Flesh and blood? Whenever I
rest at the window, when it's finished raining, and my
eyes follow the white stockings along as they hurry across
the street . . . Damnation, Woyzeck, I know what love
is, too, then! I'm made of flesh and blood, too. But,
Woyzeck: Virtue! Virtue! How was I to get rid of the
time? I always say to myself: "You're a virtuous man
[*Moved*], a good man, a good man."

Woyzeck. Yes, Captain, sir: Virtue. I haven't got much
of that. You see, us common people, we haven't got virtue.
That's the way it's got to be. But if I could be a gentleman, and if I could have a hat and a watch and a cane,
and if I could talk refined, I'd want to be virtuous, all right.
There must be something beautiful in virtue, Captain, sir.
But I'm just a poor good-for-nothing!

Captain. Good, Woyzeck. You're a good man, a good
man. But you think too much. It eats at you. You always
seem so exasperated. Our discussion has affected me
deeply. You can go now. And don't run so! Slowly! Nice
and slowly down the street!

SCENE II—*An open field. The town in the distance*

WOYZECK *and* ANDRES *cut twigs from the bushes.* ANDRES *whistles.*

WOYZECK. Andres? You know this place is cursed? Look at that light streak over there on the grass. There where the toadstools grow up. That's where the head rolls every night. One time somebody picked it up. He thought it was a hedgehog. Three days and three nights and he was in a box. [*Low.*] Andres, it was the Freemasons, don't you see, it was the Freemasons!

Andres [*sings*].
      Two little rabbits sat on a lawn
      Eating, oh, eating the green green grass . . .

Woyzeck. Quiet! Can you hear it, Andres? Can you hear it? Something moving!

Andres [*sings*].
      Eating, oh, eating the green green grass
      Till all the grass was gone.

Woyzeck. It's moving behind me! Under me! [*Stamps on the ground.*] Listen! Hollow! It's all hollow down there! It's the Freemasons!

Andres. I'm afraid.

Woyzeck. Strange how still it is. You almost want to hold your breath. Andres!

Andres. What?

Woyzeck. Say something! [*Looks about fixedly.*] Andres! How bright it is! It's all glowing over the town! A fire's sailing around the sky and a noise coming down like trumpets. It's coming closer! Let's get out of here! Don't look back! [*Drags him into the bushes.*]

Andres [*after a pause*]. Woyzeck? Do you still hear it?

Woyzeck. It's quiet now. So quiet. Like the world's dead.

Andres. Listen! I can hear the drums inside. We've got to go!

SCENE III—*The town*

MARIE *with her* CHILD *at the window.* MARGRET. *The Retreat passes,* THE DRUM MAJOR *at its head.*

MARIE [*rocking* THE CHILD *in her arms*]. Ho, boy! Da-da-da-da! Can you hear? They're coming! There!

   Margret. What a man! Built like a tree!

   Marie. He walks like a lion. [THE DRUM MAJOR *salutes* MARIE.]

   Margret. Oh, what a look he threw you, neighbor! We're not used to such things from you.

   Marie [*sings*].

         Soldiers, oh, you pretty lads . . .

   Margret. Your eyes are still shining.

   Marie. And if they are? Take *your* eyes to the Jew's and let him clean them for you. Maybe he can shine them so you can sell them for a pair of buttons!

   Margret. Look who's talking! Just look who's talking! If it isn't the Virgin herself! I'm a respectable person. But you! Everyone knows you could stare your way through seven layers of leather pants!

   Marie. Slut! [*Slams the window shut.*] Come, boy! What's it to them, anyway! Even if you are just a poor whore's baby, your dishonorable little face still makes your mother happy! [*Sings.*]

         I have my trouble and bother
         But, baby dear, where is your father?
         Why should I worry and fight
         I'll hold you and sing through the night:
         Heio popeio, my baby, my dove
         What do I want now with love?

[*A knock at the window.*] Who's there? Is it you, Franz? Come in!

   Woyzeck. Can't. There's roll call.

   Marie. Did you cut wood for the Captain?

   Woyzeck. Yes, Marie.

   Marie. What is it, Franz? You look so troubled.

   Woyzeck. Marie, it happened again, only there was

more. Isn't it written: "And there arose a smoke out of the
pit, as the smoke of a great furnace"?

Marie. Oh, Franz!

Woyzeck. Shh! Quiet! I've got it! The Freemasons!
There was a terrible noise in the sky and everything was
on fire! I'm on the trail of something, something big. It
followed me all the way to the town. Something that I
can't put my hands on, or understand. Something that
drives us mad What'll come of it all?

Marie. Franz!

Woyzeck. Don't you see? Look around you! Everything
hard and fixed, so gloomy. What's moving back there?
When God goes, everything goes. I've got to get back.

Marie. And the child?

Woyzeck. My God, the boy!—Tonight at the fair! I've
saved something again.   [*He leaves.*

Marie. That man! Seeing things like that! He'll go mad
if he keeps thinking that way! He frightened me! It's so
gloomy here. Why are you so quiet, boy? Are you afraid?
It's growing so dark. As if we were going blind. Only that
street lamp shining in from outside. [*Sings.*]

> And what if your cradle is bad
> Sleep tight, my lovey, my lad.

I can't stand it! It makes me shiver!   [*She goes out.*

SCENE IV—*Fair booths. Lights. People*

OLD MAN *with a* CHILD, WOYZECK, MARIE, CHARLATAN,
WIFE, DRUM MAJOR, *and* SERGEANT

OLD MAN [*sings while* THE CHILD *dances to the barrel-
organ*].

> There's nothing on this earth will last,
> Our lives are as the fields of grass,
> Soon all is past, is past.

Woyzeck. Ho! Hip-hop there, boy! Hip-hop! Poor man,
old man! Poor child, young child! Trouble and happiness!

Marie. My God, when fools still have their senses, then
we're all fools. Oh, what a mad world! What a beautiful
world!

They go over to THE CHARLATAN *who stands in front of a booth, his* WIFE *in trousers, and a monkey in costume*

Charlatan. Gentlemen, gentlemen! You see here before you a creature as God created it! But it is nothing this way! Absolutely nothing! But now look at what Art can do. It walks upright. Wears coat and pants. And even carries a saber. This monkey here is a regular soldier. So what if he *isn't* much different! So what if he *is* still on the bottom rung of the human ladder! Hey there, take a bow! That's the way! Now you're a baron, at least. Give us a kiss! [*The monkey trumpets.*] This little customer's musical, too. And, gentlemen, in here you will see the astronomical horse and the little lovebirds. Favorites of all the crowned heads of Europe. They'll tell you anything: how old you are, how many children you have, what your ailments are. The performance is about to begin. And at the beginning. The beginning of the beginning!

Woyzeck. You know, I had a little dog once who kept sniffing around the rim of a big hat, and I thought I'd be good to him and make it easier for him and sat him on top of it. And all the people stood around and clapped.

Gentlemen. Oh, grotesque! How really grotesque!

Woyzeck. Don't you believe in God either? It's an honest fact I don't believe in God.—You call that grotesque? I like what's grotesque. See that? That grotesque enough for you?—[*To* MARIE.] You want to go in?

Marie. Sure. That must be nice in there. Look at the tassels on him! And his wife's got pants on!

[*They go inside.*

Drum Major. Wait a minute! Did you see her? What a piece!

Sergeant. Hell, she could whelp a couple regiments of cavalry!

Drum Major. And breed drum majors!

Sergeant. Look at the way she carries that head! You'd think all that black hair would pull her down like a weight. And those eyes!

Drum Major. Like looking down a well . . . or up a chimney. Come on, let's go after her!

SCENE V—*Interior of the brightly lighted booth*

MARIE, WOYZECK, PROPRIETOR OF THE BOOTH, SERGEANT,
and DRUM MAJOR

MARIE. All these lights!

Woyzeck. Sure, Marie. Black cats with fiery eyes.

Proprietor of the Booth [*bringing forward a horse*]. Show your talent! Show your brute reason! Put human society to shame! Gentlemen, this animal you see here, with a tail on its torso, and standing on its four hoofs, is a member of all the learnèd societies—as well as a professor at our university where he teaches students how to ride and fight. But that requires simple intelligence. Now think with your double reason! What do you do when you think with your double reason? Is there a jackass in this learnèd assembly? [*The nag shakes its head.*] How's that for double reasoning? That's physiognomy for you. This is no dumb animal. This is a person! A human being! But still an animal. A beast. [*The nag conducts itself indecently.*] That's right, put society to shame. As you can see, this animal is still in a state of Nature. Not ideal Nature, of course! Take a lesson from him! But ask your doctor first, it may prove highly dangerous! What we have been told by this is: Man must be natural! You are created of dust, sand, and dung. Why must you be more than dust, sand, and dung? Look there at his reason. He can figure even if he can't count it off on his fingers. And why? Because he cannot express himself, can't explain. A metamorphosed human being. Tell the gentlemen what time it is! Which of you ladies and gentlemen has a watch? A watch?

Sergeant. A watch? [*He pulls a watch imposingly and measuredly from his pocket.*] There you are, my good man!

Marie. I want to see this. [*She clambers down to the first row of seats;* THE SERGEANT *helps her.*]

Drum Major. What a piece!

SCENE VI—MARIE's *room*

MARIE *with her* CHILD

MARIE [*sitting, her* CHILD *on her lap, a piece of mirror in her hand*]. He told Franz to get the hell out, so what could he do! [*Looks at herself in the mirror.*] Look how the stones shine! What kind are they, I wonder? What kind did he say they were? Sleep, boy! Close your eyes! Tight! Stay that way now. Don't move or he'll get you. [*Sings.*]

> Hurry, lady, close up tight
> A gypsy lad is out tonight
> And he will take you by the hand
> And lead you into gypsyland.

[*Continues to look at herself in the mirror.*] They must be gold! I wonder how they'll look on me at the dance! Our kind's got only a little corner in the world and a piece of broken mirror. But my mouth is just as red as any of the fine ladies with their mirrors from top to bottom, and their handsome gentlemen that kiss their hands for them! I'm just a poor common piece! [THE CHILD *sits up.*] Quiet, boy! Close your eyes! There's the sandman! Look at him run across the wall! [*She flashes with the mirror.*] Eyes tight! Or he'll look into them and make you blind!

WOYZECK *enters behind her. She jumps up, her hands at her ears.*

Woyzeck. What's that?
Marie. Nothing.
Woyzeck. There's something shiny in your hands.
Marie. An earring. I found it.
Woyzeck. I never have luck like that! Two at a time!
Marie. Am I human or not?
Woyzeck. I'm sorry, Marie.—Look at the boy asleep. Lift his arm, the chair's hurting him. Look at the shiny drops on his forehead. Everything under the sun works! We even sweat in our sleep. Us poor people! Here's some

money again, Marie. My pay and something from the
Captain.

Marie. God bless you, Franz.

Woyzeck. I've got to get back. Tonight, Marie! I'll see
you tonight!   [*He goes off.*

Marie [*alone, after a pause*]. I *am* bad, I *am!* I could
run myself through with a knife! Oh, what a life, what
a life! We'll all end up in hell, anyway, in the end: man,
woman, and child!

SCENE VII—*At the* DOCTOR'S

THE DOCTOR *and* WOYZECK

DOCTOR. I don't believe it, Woyzeck! And a man of your
word!

Woyzeck. What's that, Doctor, sir?

Doctor. I saw it all, Woyzeck. You pissed on the street!
You were pissing on the wall like a dog! And here I'm
giving you three groschen a day plus board! That's terrible, Woyzeck! The world's becoming a terrible place,
a terrible place!

Woyzeck. But, Doctor, sir, when Nature . . .

Doctor. When Nature? When Nature? What has
Nature to do with it? Did I or did I not prove to you that
the *musculus constrictor vesicae* is controlled by your
will? Nature! Woyzeck, man is free! In Mankind alone
we see glorified the individual's will to freedom! And you
couldn't hold your water! [*Shakes his head, places his
hands behind the small of his back, and walks back and
forth.*] Have you eaten your peas today, Woyzeck? Nothing
but peas! *Cruciferae!* Remember that! There's going to be
a revolution in science! I'm going to blow it sky-high!
Urea Oxygen. Ammonium hydrochloratem hyperoxidic.
Woyzeck, couldn't you just *try* to piss again? Go in the
other room there and make another try.

Woyzeck. Doctor, sir, I can't.

Doctor [*disturbed*]. But you could piss on the wall. I
have it here in black and white. Our contract is right
here! I saw it. I saw it with these very eyes. I had just
stuck my head out the window, opening it to let in the

rays of the sun, so as to execute the process of sneezing.
[*Going toward him.*] No, Woyzeck, I'm not going to vex
myself. Vexation is unhealthy. Unscientific. I'm calm now,
completely calm. My pulse is beating at its accustomed
sixty, and I am speaking to you in utmost cold-bloodedness. Why should I vex myself over a man, God forbid!
A man! Now if he were a Proteus, it would be worth the
vexation! But, Woyzeck, you really shouldn't have pissed
on the wall.

Woyzeck. You see, Doctor, sir, sometimes a person's
got a certain kind of character, like when he's made a certain way. But with Nature it's not the same, you see.
With Nature [*He snaps his fingers.*], it's like *that!* How
should I explain, it's like——

Doctor. Woyzeck, you're philosophizing again.

Woyzeck [*confidingly*]. Doctor, sir, did you ever see
anything with double nature? Like when the sun stops
at noon, and it's like the world was going up in fire? That's
when I hear a terrible voice saying things to me!

Doctor. Woyzeck, you have an *aberratio!*

Woyzeck [*places his finger at his nose*]. It's in the toadstools, Doctor, sir, that's where it is. Did you ever see
the shapes the toadstools make when they grow up out
of the earth? If only somebody could read what they say!

Doctor. Woyzeck, you have a most beautiful *aberratio
mentalis partialis* of a secondary order! And so wonderfully developed! Woyzeck, your salary is increased! *Idée
fixe* of a secondary order, and with a generally rational
state. You go about your business normally? Still shaving
the Captain?

Woyzeck. Yes, sir.

Doctor. You eat your peas?

Woyzeck. Just as always, Doctor, sir. My wife gets the
money for the household.

Doctor. Still in the army?

Woyzeck. Yes, sir, Doctor.

Doctor. You're an interesting case. Patient Woyzeck,
you're to have an increase in salary. So behave yourself!
Let's feel the pulse. Ah yes.

SCENE VIII—MARIE's *room*

DRUM MAJOR *and* MARIE

DRUM MAJOR. Marie!

Marie [looking at him, with expression]. Go on, show me how you march!—Chest broad as a bull's and a beard like a lion! There's not another man in the world like that! And there's not a prouder woman than me!

Drum Major. Wait till Sunday when I wear my helmet with the plume and my white gloves! Damn, that'll be a sight for you! The Prince always says: "My God, there goes a real man!"

Marie [scoffing]. Ha! [*Goes toward him.*] A man?

Drum Major. You're not such a bad piece yourself! Hell, we'll plot a whole brood of drum majors! Right? [*He puts his arm around her.*]

Marie [annoyed]. Let go!

Drum Major. Bitch!

Marie [fiercely]. You just touch me!

Drum Major. There's devils in your eyes.

Marie. Let there be, for all I care! What's the difference!

SCENE IX—*Street*

CAPTAIN *and* DOCTOR. THE CAPTAIN *comes panting along the street, stops; pants, looks about.*

CAPTAIN. Ho, Doctor, don't run so fast! Don't paddle the air so with your stick! You're only courting death that way! A good man with a good conscience never walks as fast as that. A good man . . . [*He catches him by the coat.*] Doctor, permit me to save a human life!

Doctor. I'm in a hurry, Captain, I'm in a hurry!

Captain. Doctor, I'm so melancholy. I have such fantasies. I start to cry every time I see my coat hanging on the wall.

Doctor. Hm! Bloated, fat, thick neck: apoplectic constitution. Yes, Captain, you'll be having *apoplexia cerebria* any time now. Of course you could have it on only one side. In which case you'll be paralyzed down that one side. Or if things go really well you'll be mentally disabled so that you can vegetate away for the rest of your days. You may look forward to something approximately like that within the next four weeks! And, furthermore, I can assure you that you give promise of being a most interesting case. And if it is God's will that only one half of your tongue become paralyzed, then we will conduct the most immortal of experiments.

Captain. Doctor, you mustn't scare me that way! People are said to have died of fright. Of pure, sheer fright. I can see them now with lemons in their hands. But they'll say: "He was a good man, a good man." You devil's coffinnail-maker!

Doctor [*extending his hat toward him*]. Do you know who this is, Captain? This is Sir Hollowhead, my most honorable Captain Drilltheirassesoff!

Captain [*makes a series of folds in his sleeve*]. And do you know who this is, Doctor? This is Sir Manifold, my dear devil's coffinnail-maker! Ha! Ha! Ha! But no harm meant! I'm a good man, but I can play, too, when I want to, Doctor, when I want to . . .

WOYZECK *comes toward them and tries to pass in a hurry.*

Captain. Ho! Woyzeck! Where are you off to in such a hurry? Stay awhile, Woyzeck! Running through the world like an open razor, you're liable to cut someone. He runs as if he had to shave a castrated regiment and would be hung before he discovered and cut the longest hair that wasn't there. But on the subject of long beards . . . What was it I wanted to say? Woyzeck, why was I thinking about beards?

Doctor. The wearing of long beards on the chin, remarks Pliny, is a habit of which soldiers must be broken——

Captain [*continues*]. Ah, yes, this thing about beards! Tell me, Woyzeck, have you found any long hairs from beards in your soup bowl lately? Ho, I don't think he understands! A hair from a human face, from the beard of

an engineer, a sergeant, a . . . a drum major? Well,
Woyzeck? But then he's got a good wife. It's not the
same as with the others.

Woyzeck. Yes, sir, Captain! What was it you wanted to
say to me, Captain, sir?

Captain. What a face he's making! Well, maybe not
in his soup, but if he hurries home around the corner
I'll wager he might still find one on a certain pair of lips.
A pair of lips, Woyzeck. I know what love is, too, Woyzeck. Look at him, he's white as chalk!

Woyzeck. Captain, sir, I'm just a poor devil. And
there's nothing else I've got in the world but her. Captain, sir, if you're just making a fool of me . . .

Captain. A fool? Me? Making a fool of you, Woyzeck?

Doctor. Your pulse, Woyzeck, your pulse! Short, hard,
skipping, irregular.

Woyzeck. Captain, sir, the earth's hot as coals in hell.
But I'm cold as ice, cold as ice. Hell is cold. I'll bet you.
I don't believe it! God! God! I don't believe it!

Captain. Look here, you, how would you . . . how'd you
like a pair of bullets in your skull? You keep stabbing at
me with those eyes of yours, and I'm only trying to help.
Because you're a good man, Woyzeck, a good man.

Doctor. Facial muscles rigid, taut, occasionally twitches.
Condition strained, excitable.

Woyzeck. I'm going. Anything's possible. The bitch!
Anything's possible.—The weather's nice, Captain, sir.
Look, a beautiful, hard, gray sky. You'd almost like to
pound a nail in up there and hang yourself on it. And
only because of that little dash between Yes and Yes
again . . . and No. Captain, sir: Yes and No: did No
make Yes or Yes make No? I must think about that.

*He goes off with long strides, slowly at first, then faster
and faster.*

Doctor [*shouting after him*]. Phenomenon! Woyzeck,
you get a raise!

Captain. I get so dizzy around such people. Look at
him go! Long-legged rascals like him step out like a
shadow running away from its own spider. But short ones

only dawdle along. The long-legged ones are the lightning, the short ones the thunder. Haha . . . Grotesque!
Grotesque!

SCENE X—MARIE'S *room*

WOYZECK *and* MARIE

WOYZECK [*looks fixedly at her and shakes his head*]. Hm!
I don't see it! I don't see it! My God, why can't I see it,
why can't I take it in my fists!

Marie [*frightened*]. Franz, what is it?—You're raving,
Franz.

Woyzeck. A sin so swollen and big—it stinks to smoke
the angels out of Heaven! You have a red mouth, Marie!
No blisters on it? Marie, you're beautiful as sin. How can
mortal sin be so beautiful?

Marie. Franz, it's your fever making you talk this way!

Woyzeck. Damn you! Is this where he stood? Like this?
Like this?

Marie. While the day's long and the world's old a lot
of people can stand in one spot, one right after the other.
—Why are you looking at me so strange, Franz! I'm
afraid!

Woyzeck. It's a nice street for walking, uh? You could
walk corns on your feet! It's nice walking on the street,
going around in society.

Marie. Society?

Woyzeck. A lot of people pass through this street here,
don't they! And you talk to them—to whoever you want—
but that's not my business!—Why wasn't it me!

Marie. You expect me to tell people to keep off the
streets—and take their mouths with them when they
leave?

Woyzeck. And don't you ever leave your lips at home,
they're too beautiful, it would be a sin! But then I guess
the wasps like to light on them, uh?

Marie. And what wasp stung you! You're like a cow
chased by hornets!

Woyzeck. I saw him!

Marie. You can see a lot with two eyes while the sun
shines!

Woyzeck. Whore! [*He goes after her.*]

Marie. Don't you touch me, Franz! I'd rather have a knife in my body than your hands touch me. When I looked at him, my father didn't dare lay a hand on me from the time I was ten.

Woyzeck. Whore! No, it should show on you! Something! Every man's a chasm. It makes you dizzy when you look down in. It's got to show! And she looks like innocence itself. So, innocence, there's a spot on you. But I can't prove it—can't prove it! Who can prove it?

[*He goes off.*

SCENE XI—*The guardhouse*

WOYZECK *and* ANDRES

ANDRES [*sings*].
> Our hostess she has a pretty maid
> She sits in her garden night and day
> She sits within her garden . . .

Woyzeck. Andres!

Andres. Hm?

Woyzeck. Nice weather.

Andres. Sunday weather.—They're playing music tonight outside the town. All the whores are already there. The men stinking and sweating. Wonderful, uh?

Woyzeck [*restlessly*]. They're dancing, Andres, they're dancing!

Andres. Sure. So what? [*Sings.*]
> She sits within her garden
> But when the bells have tollèd
> Then she waits at her garden gate
> Or so the soldiers say.

Woyzeck. Andres, I can't keep quiet.

Andres. You're a fool!

Woyzeck. I've got to go out there. It keeps turning and turning in my head. They're dancing, dancing! Will she have hot hands, Andres? God damn her, Andres! God damn her!

Andres. What do you want?

Woyzeck. I've got to go out there. I've got to see them.

Andres. Aren't you ever satisfied? What's all this for a whore?

Woyzeck. I've got to get out of here! I can't stand the heat!

SCENE XII—*The inn*

The windows are open. Dancing. Benches in front of the inn. APPRENTICES

FIRST APPRENTICE [*sings*].
> This shirt I've got on, it is not mine
> And my soul it stinketh of brandywine . . .

Second Apprentice. Brother, let me be a real friend and knock a hole in your nature! Forward! I'll knock a hole in his nature! Hell, I'm as good a man as he is; I'll kill every flea on his body!

First Apprentice. My soul, my soul stinketh of brandy-wine!—And even money passeth into decay! Forget me not, but the world's a beautiful place! Brother, my sadness could fill a barrel with tears! I wish our noses were two bottles so we could pour them down one another's throats.

The Others [*in chorus*].
> A hunter from the Rhine
> Once rode through a forest so fine
> Hallei-hallo, he called to me
> From high on a meadow, open and free
> A hunter's life for me.

WOYZECK *stands at the window.* MARIE *and* THE DRUM MAJOR *dance past without noticing him.*

Woyzeck. Both of them! God damn her!

Marie [*dancing past*]. Don't stop! Don't stop!

Woyzeck [*seats himself on the bench, trembling, as he looks from there through the window*]. Listen! Listen! Ha, roll on each other, roll and turn! Don't stop, don't stop, she says!

Idiot. Pah! It stinks!

Woyzeck. Yes, it stinks! Her cheeks are red, red, why should she stink already? Karl, what is it you smell?

Idiot. I smell, I smell blood.

Woyzeck. Blood? Why are all things red that I look at now? Why are they all rolling in a sea of blood, one on top of the other, tumbling, tumbling! Ha, the sea is red!—Don't stop! Don't stop! [*He starts up passionately, then sinks down again onto the bench.*] Don't stop! Don't stop! [*Beating his hands together.*] Turn and roll and roll and turn! God, blow out the sun and let them roll on each other in their lechery! Man and woman and man and beast! They'll do it in the light of the sun! They'll do it in the palm of your hand like flies! Whore! That whore's red as coals, red as coals! Don't stop! Don't stop! [*Jumps up.*] Watch how the bastard takes hold of her! Touching her body! He's holding her now, holding her . . . the way I held her once. [*He slumps down in a stupor.*]

First Apprentice [*preaching from a table*]. I say unto you, forget not the wanderer who standeth leaning against the stream of time, and who giveth himself answer with the wisdom of God, and saith: What is Man? What is Man? Yea, verily I say unto you: How should the farmer, the cooper, the shoemaker, the doctor, live, had not God created Man for their use? How should the tailor live had not God endowed Man with the need to slaughter himself? And therefore doubt ye not, for all things are lovely and sweet! Yet the world with all its things is an evil place, and even money passeth into decay. In conclusion, my belovèd brethren, let us piss once more upon the Cross so that somewhere a Jew will die!

Amid the general shouting and laughing WOYZECK *wakens.* PEOPLE *are leaving the inn.*

Andres. What are you doing there?

Woyzeck. What time is it?

Andres. Ten.

Woyzeck. Is that all it is? I think it should go faster— I want to think about it before night.

Andres. Why?

Woyzeck. So it'd be over.

Andres. What?

Woyzeck. The fun.

Andres. What are you sitting here by the door for?

Woyzeck. Because it feels good, and because I know—
a lot of people sit by doors, but they don't know—they
don't know till they're dragged out of the door feet first.

Andres. Come with me!

Woyzeck. It feels good here like this—and even better
if I laid myself down . . .

Andres. There's blood on your head.

Woyzeck. In my head, maybe.—If they all knew what
time it was they'd strip themselves naked and put on a
silk shirt and let the carpenter make their bed of wood
shavings.

Andres. He's drunk.

Goes off with the others.

Woyzeck. The world is out of order! Why did the
street-lamp cleaner forget to wipe my eyes—everything's
dark. Devil damn you, God! I lay in my own way: jump
over myself. Where's my shadow gone? There's no safety
in the kennels any more. Shine the moon through my legs
again to see if my shadow's here. [*Sings.*]

> Eating, oh, eating the green green grass
> Eating, oh, eating the green green grass
> Till all the grass was go-o-one.

What's that lying over there? Shining like that? It's making me look. How it sparkles. I've got to have it.

[*He rushes off.*

SCENE XIII—An open field

WOYZECK

WOYZECK. Don't stop! Don't stop! Hishh! Hashh! That's
how the fiddles and pipes go.—Don't stop! Don't stop!
—Stop your playing! What's that talking down there?
[*He stretches out on the ground.*] What? What are you
saying? What? Louder! Louder! Stab? Stab the goat-
bitch dead? Stab? Stab her? The goat-bitch dead? Should
I? Must I? Do I hear it there, too? Does the wind say so,
too? Won't it ever stop, ever stop? Stab her! Stab her!
Dead! Dead!

SCENE XIV—*A room in the barracks. Night*

ANDRES *and* WOYZECK *in a bed.*

WOYZECK [*softly.*] Andres! [ANDRES *murmurs in his sleep.
Shakes* ANDRES.] Andres! Hey, Andres!

Andres. Mmmmm! What do you want?

Woyzeck. I can't sleep! When I close my eyes everything turns and turns. I hear voices in the fiddles: Don't
stop! Don't stop! And then the walls start to talk. Can't
you hear it?

Andres. Sure. Let them dance! I'm tired. God bless us
all, Amen.

Woyzeck. It's always saying: Stab! Stab! And then when
I close my eyes it keeps shining there, a big, broad knife,
on a table by a window in a narrow, dark street, and an
old man sitting behind it. And the knife is always in front
of my eyes.

Andres. Go to sleep, you fool!

Woyzeck. Andres! There's something outside. In the
ground. They're always pointing to it. Don't you hear
them now, listen, now, knocking on the walls? Somebody
must have seen me out the window. Don't you hear?
I hear it all day long. Don't stop. Stab! Stab the——

Andres. Lay down. You ought to go to the hospital.
They'll give you a schnapps with a powder in it. It'll cut
your fever.

Woyzeck. Don't stop! Don't stop!

Andres. Go to sleep!

He goes back to sleep.

SCENE XV—THE DOCTOR'S *courtyard*

STUDENTS *and* WOYZECK *below,* THE DOCTOR *in the
attic window.*

DOCTOR. Gentlemen, I find myself on the roof like David
when he beheld Bathsheba. But all I see are the Parisian
panties of the girls' boarding school drying in the garden.

Gentlemen, we are concerned with the weighty question of the relationship of the subject to the object. If, for example, we were to take one of those innumerable things in which we see the highest manifestation of the self-affirmation of the Godhead, and examine its relationship to space, to the earth, and to the planetary constellations . . . Gentlemen, if we were to take this cat and toss it out the window: how would this object conduct itself in conformity with its own instincts towards its *centrum gravitationis?* Well, Woyzeck? [*Roars.*] Woyzeck!

Woyzeck [*picks up the cat*]. Doctor, sir, she's biting me!

Doctor. Damn, why do you handle the beast so tenderly! It's not your grandmother! [*He descends.*]

Woyzeck. Doctor, I'm shaking.

Doctor [*utterly delighted*]. Excellent, Woyzeck, excellent! [*Rubs his hands, takes the cat.*] What's this, gentlemen? The new species of rabbit louse! A beautiful species . . . [*He pulls out a magnifying glass; the cat runs off.*] Animals, gentlemen, simply have no scientific instincts. But in its place you may see something else. Now, observe: for three months this man has eaten nothing but peas. Notice the effect. Feel how irregularly his pulse beats! And look at his eyes!

Woyzeck. Doctor, sir, everything's going dark! [*He sits down.*]

Doctor. Courage, Woyzeck! A few more days and then it will all be over with. Feel, gentlemen, feel! [*They fumble over his temples, pulse, and chest.*]

Doctor. Apropos, Woyzeck, wiggle your ears for the gentlemen! I've meant to show you this before. He uses only two muscles. Let's go, let's go! You stupid animal, shall I wiggle them for you? Trying to run out on us like the cat? There you are, gentlemen! Here you see an example of the transition into a donkey: frequently the result of being raised by women and of a persistent usage of the Germanic language. How much hair has your mother pulled out recently for sentimental remembrances of you? It's become so thin these last few days. It's the peas, gentlemen, the peas!

SCENE XVI—*The inn*

WOYZECK. THE SERGEANT

WOYZECK [*sings*].
> Oh, daughter, my daughter
> And didn't you know
> That sleeping with coachmen
> Would bring you low?

What is it that our Good Lord God cannot do? What? He cannot make what is done undone. Ha! Ha! Ha!— But that's the way it is, and that's the way it should be. But to make things better is to make things better. And a respectable man loves his life, and a man who loves his life has no courage, and a virtuous man has no courage. A man with courage is a dirty dog.

Sergeant [*with dignity*]. You're forgetting yourself in the presence of a brave man.

Woyzeck. I wasn't talking about anybody, I wasn't talking about anything, not like the Frenchmen do when they talk, but it was good of you.—But a man with courage is a dirty dog.

Sergeant. Damn you! You broken mustache cup! You watch or I'll see you drink a pot of your own piss and swallow your own razor!

Woyzeck. Sir, you do yourself an injustice! Was it *you* I talked about? Did I say *you* had courage? Don't torment me, sir! My name is science. Every week for my scientific career I get half a guilder. You mustn't cut me in two or I'll go hungry. I'm a *Spinosa pericyclia*; I have a Latin behind. I am a living skeleton. All Mankind studies me. —What is Man? Bones! Dust, sand, dung. What is Nature? Dust, sand, dung. But poor, stupid Man, stupid Man! We must be friends. If only you had no courage, there would be no science. Only Nature, no amputation, no articulation. What is this? Woyzeck's arm, flesh, bones, veins. What is this? Dung. Why is it rooted in dung? Must I cut off my arm? No, Man is selfish, he beats, shoots, stabs his own kind. [*He sobs.*] We must be friends. I wish our noses were two bottles that we could pour down each other's throats. What a beautiful place the world is! Friend! My friend! The world! [*Moved.*] Look! The sun coming through the clouds—like God emptying His bedpan on the world. [*He cries.*]

SCENE XVII—*The barracks yard*

WOYZECK. ANDRES

WOYZECK. What have you heard?

Andres. He's still inside with a friend.

Woyzeck. He said something.

Andres. How do you know? Why do I have to be the one to tell you? Well, he laughed and then he said she was some piece. And then something or other about her thighs—and that she was hot as a red poker.

Woyzeck [*quite coldly*]. So, he said that? What was that I dreamed about last night? About a knife? What stupid dreams we get!

Andres. Hey, friend! Where you off to?

Woyzeck. Get some wine for the Captain. Andres, you know something? There aren't many girls like she was.

Andres. Like who was?

Woyzeck. Nothing. I'll see you.   [*Goes off.*

SCENE XVIII—*The inn*

DRUM MAJOR, WOYZECK, *and* PEOPLE

DRUM MAJOR. I'm a man! [*He pounds his chest.*] A man, you hear? Anybody say different? Anybody who's not as crocked as the Lord God Himself better keep off. I'll screw his nose up his own ass! I'll . . . [*To* WOYZECK.] You there, get drunk! I wish the world was schnapps, schnapps! You better start drinking! [WOYZECK *whistles.*] Son-of-a-bitch, you want me to pull your tongue out and wrap it around your middle? [*They wrestle;* WOYZECK *loses.*] You want I should leave enough wind in you for a good old lady's fart? Uh! [*Exhausted and trembling,* WOYZECK *seats himself on the bench.*] The son-of-a-bitch can whistle himself blue in the face for all I care. [*Sings.*]

> Brandy's all my life, my life
> Brandy gives me courage!

A Man. He sure got more than he asked for.

Another. He's bleeding.

Woyzeck. One thing after another.

SCENE XIX—*Pawnbroker's shop*

WOYZECK *and* THE JEW

Woyzeck. The pistol costs too much.

Jew. So you want it or not? Make up your mind.

Woyzeck. How much was the knife?

Jew. It's straight and sharp. What do you want it for? To cut your throat? So what's the matter? You get it as cheap here as anywhere else. You'll die cheap enough, but not for nothing. What's the matter? It'll be a cheap death.

Woyzeck. This'll cut more than bread.

Jew. Two groschen.

Woyzeck. There!   [*He goes out.*

Jew. There, he says! Like it was nothing! And it's real money!—Dog!

SCENE XX—MARIE's *room*

THE IDIOT. THE CHILD. MARIE

Idiot [*lying down, telling fairy tales on his fingers*]. This one has the golden crown. He's the Lord King. Tomorrow I'll bring the Lady Queen her child. Bloodsausage says: Come, Liversausage . . .

Marie [*paging through her Bible*]. "And no guile is found in his mouth." Lord God, Lord God! Don't look at me! [*Paging further.*] "And the Scribes and Pharisees brought unto him a woman taken in adultery, and set her in the midst . . . And Jesus said unto her: Neither do I condemn thee; go, and sin no more." [*Striking her hands together.*] Lord God! Lord God! I can't. Lord God, give me only so much strength that I may pray. [THE CHILD *presses himself close to her.*] The child is a sword in my heart. [*To* THE IDIOT.] Karl!—I've strutted it in the light of the sun, like the whore I am—my sin, my sin! [THE IDIOT *takes* THE CHILD *and grows quiet.*] Franz hasn't come. Not yesterday. Not today. It's getting hot in here! [*She opens the window and reads further.*] "And stood at his feet weeping, and began to wash his feet with tears, and did wipe them with the hairs of her head, and anointed them with ointment." [*Striking her breast.*] Everything dead! Saviour! Saviour! If only I might anoint Your feet!

SCENE XXI—*An open field*

WOYZECK

WOYZECK [*buries the knife in a hole*]. Thou shalt not kill. Lay here! I can't stay here!   [*He rushes off.*

SCENE XXII—*The barracks*

ANDRES. WOYZECK *rummages through his belongings.*

WOYZECK. Andres, this jacket's not part of the uniform, but you can use it, Andres.
    Andres [*replies numbly to almost everything with*]. Sure.
    WOYZECK. The cross is my sister's. And the ring.
    Andres. Sure.
    WOYZECK. I've got a Holy Picture, too: two hearts—they're real gold. I found it in my mother's Bible, and it said:

O Lord with wounded head so sore
So may my heart be evermore.

My mother only feels now when the sun shines on her hands . . . that doesn't matter.
    Andres. Sure.
    WOYZECK [*pulls out a paper*]. Friedrich Johann Franz Woyzeck. Soldier. Rifleman, Second Regiment, Second Battalion, Fourth Company. Born: the Feast of the Annunciation, twentieth of July. Today I'm thirty years old, seven months and twelve days.
    Andres. Go to the hospital, Franz. Poor guy, you've

got to drink some schnapps with a powder in it. It'll kill the fever.

Woyzeck. You know, Andres—when the carpenter puts those boards together, nobody knows who it's made for.

SCENE XXIII—*The street*

MARIE *with little* GIRLS *in front of the house door.*
GRANDMOTHER. *Later* WOYZECK

GIRLS [*singing*].
> The sun shone bright on Candlemas Day
> And the corn was all in bloom
> And they marched along the meadow way
> They marched by two and two.
> The pipers marched ahead
> The fiddlers followed through
> And their socks were scarlet red . . .

First Child. I don't like that one.
Second Child. Why do you always want to be different?
First Child. You sing for us, Marie!
Marie. I can't.
Second Child. Why?
Marie. Because.
Second Child. But *why* because?
Third Child. Grandmother, *you* tell us a story!
Grandmother. All right, you little crab apples!—Once upon a time there was a poor little girl who had no father and no mother. Everyone was dead, and there was no one left in the whole wide world. Everyone was dead. And the little girl went out and looked for someone night and day. And because there was no one left on the earth, she wanted to go to Heaven. And the moon looked down so friendly at her. And when she finally got to the moon, it was a piece of rotten wood. And so she went to the sun, and it was a faded sunflower. And when she got to the stars, they were little golden flies, stuck up there as if they were caught in a spider's web. And when she wanted to go back to earth, the earth was an upside-down pot. And she was all alone. And she sat down there and she cried. And she sits there to this day, all, all alone.

Woyzeck [appears]. Marie!
Marie [startled]. What!
Woyzeck. Let's go. It's getting time.
Marie. Where to?
Woyzeck. How should I know?

SCENE XXIV—*A pond by the edge of the woods*

MARIE *and* WOYZECK

MARIE. Then the town must be out that way. It's so dark.
Woyzeck. You can't go yet. Come, sit down.
Marie. But I've got to get back.
Woyzeck. You don't want to run your feet sore.
Marie. What's happened to you?
Woyzeck. You know how long it's been, Marie?
Marie. Two years from Pentecost.
Woyzeck. You know how much longer it'll last?
Marie. I've got to get back. Supper's not made yet.
Woyzeck. Are you freezing, Marie? And still you're so
warm. Your lips are hot as coals! Hot as coals, the hot
breath of a whore! And still I'd give up Heaven just to
kiss them again. Are you freezing? When you're cold
through, you won't freeze any more. The morning dew
won't freeze you.
Marie. What are you talking about?
Woyzeck. Nothing. *[Silence.]*
Marie. Look how red the moon is! It's rising.
Woyzeck. Like a knife washed in blood.
Marie. What are you going to do? Franz, you're so
pale. *[He raises the knife.]*
Marie. Franz! Stop! For Heaven's sake! Help me! Help
me!
Woyzeck [stabbing madly]. There! There! Why can't
you die? There! There! Ha, she's still shivering! Still not
dead? Still not dead? Still shivering? *[Stabbing at her
again.]* Are you dead? Dead! Dead!
                     [He drops the knife and runs away.

Two MEN *approach.*

First Man. Wait!
Second Man. You hear something? Shh! Over there!

First Man. Whhh! There! What a sound!

Second Man. It's the water, it's calling. It's a long time since anyone drowned here. Let's go! I don't like hearing such sounds!

First Man. Whhh! There it is again! Like a person, dying!

Second Man. It's uncanny! So foggy, nothing but gray mist as far as you can see—and the hum of beetles like broken bells. Let's get out of here!

First Man. No, it's too clear, it's too loud! Let's go up this way! Come on!   [*They hurry on.*

SCENE XXV—*The inn*

WOYZECK, KATHY, INNKEEPER, IDIOT, *and* PEOPLE

WOYZECK. Dance! Everybody! Don't stop! Sweat and stink! He'll get you all in the end! [*Sings.*]

> Oh, daughter, my daughter
> And didn't you know
> That sleeping with coachmen
> Would bring you low?

[*He dances.*] Ho, Kathy! Sit down! I'm so hot, so hot! [*Takes off his coat.*] That's the way it is: the devil takes one and lets the other get away. Kathy, you're hot as coals! Why, tell me why? Kathy, you'll be cold one day, too. Be reasonable.—Can't you sing something?

Kathy [*sings*].

> That Swabian land I cannot bear
> And dresses long I will not wear
> For dresses long and pointed shoes
> Are clothes a chambermaid never should choose.

Woyzeck. No shoes, no shoes! We can get to hell without shoes.

Kathy [*sings*].

> To such and like I'll not be prone
> Take back your gold and sleep alone.

Woyzeck. Sure, sure! What do I want to get all bloody for?

Kathy. Then what's that on your hand?

Woyzeck. Me? Me?

Kathy. Red! It's blood! [PEOPLE *gather round him*.]
Woyzeck. Blood? Blood?
Innkeeper. Blood!
Woyzeck. I think I cut myself. Here, on my right hand.
Innkeeper. Then why is there blood on your elbow?
Woyzeck. I wiped it off.
Innkeeper. Your right hand and you wiped it on your right elbow? You're a smart one!
Idiot. And then the Giant said: "I smell, I smell the flesh of Man." Pew, it stinks already!
Woyzeck. What do you want from me? Is it your business? Out of my way or the first one who . . . Damn you! Do I look like I murdered somebody? Do I look like a murderer? What are you looking at? Look at yourselves! Look! Out of my way!   [*He runs off.*

SCENE XXVI—*At the pond*

WOYZECK, *alone*.

WOYZECK. The knife! Where's the knife? I left it here. It'll give me away! Closer! And closer! What is this place? What's that noise? Something's moving! It's quiet now. —It's got to be here, close to her. Marie? Ha, Marie! Quiet. Everything's quiet! Why are you so pale, Marie? Why are you wearing those red beads around your neck? Who was it gave you that necklace for sinning with him? Your sins made you black, Marie, they made you black! Did I make you so pale? Why is your hair uncombed? Did you forget to twist your braids today? The knife, the knife! I've got it! There! [*He runs toward the water.*] There, into the water! [*He throws the knife into the water.*] It dives like a stone into the black water. No, it's not out far enough for when they swim! [*He wades into the pond and throws it out farther.*] There! Now! But in the summer when they dive for mussels? Ha, it'll get rusty, who'll ever notice it! Why didn't I break it first! Am I still bloody? I've got to wash myself. There, there's a spot, and there's another . . . [*He goes farther out into the water.*]

scene xxvii—*The street*

Children

First Child. Let's go find Marie!

Second Child. What happened?

First Child. Don't you know? Everybody's out there. They found a body!

Second Child. Where?

First Child. By the pond, out in the woods.

Second Child. Hurry, so we can still see something. Before they bring it back.   [*They rush off.*

scene xxviii—*In front of* Marie's *house*

Idiot. Child. Woyzeck.

Idiot [*holding* The Child *on his knee, points to* Woyzeck *as he enters*]. Looky there, he fell in the water, he fell in the water, he fell in the water!

Woyzeck. Boy! Christian!

Idiot [*looks at him fixedly*]. He fell in the water.

Woyzeck [*wanting to embrace* The Child *tenderly, but it turns from him and screams*]. My God! My God!

Idiot. He fell in the water.

Woyzeck. I'll buy you a horsey, Christian. There, there. [The Child *pulls away. To the* Idiot]. Here, buy the boy a horsey! [The Idiot *stares at him.*] Hop! Hop! Hip-hop, horsey!

Idiot [*shouting joyously*]. Hop! Hop! Hip-hop, horsey! Hip-hop, horsey!

He runs off with The Child. Woyzeck *is alone.*

scene xxix—*The morgue*

Judge, Court Clerk, Policeman, Captain, Doctor, Drum Major, Sergeant, Idiot, *and others.* Woyzeck

Policeman. What a murder! A good, genuine, beautiful

murder! Beautiful a murder as you could hope for! It's been a long time since we had one like this!

WOYZECK *stands in their midst, dumbly looking at the body of* MARIE; *he is bound, the dogmatic atheist, tall, haggard, timid, good-natured, scientific.*

LENZ

❧

LENZ

On the twentieth of January Lenz went through the mountains. The summits and high slopes were in snow, the valleys below were gray stone, green meadows, rocks, and firs.

It was cold and damp; the water trickled down the rocks and leapt across the road. The branches of the firs hung down heavily in the damp air. Gray clouds drifted across the sky, but quite close together—and then the mist rose up and swept heavily and damply through the foliage, languidly, awkwardly.

He continued on his way unconcerned; up one hill, down another, nothing to hinder his progress. He felt no sense of fatigue, except that at times he grew irritated at not being able to walk on his hands.

At first he felt oppressed as the rocks opened in front of him, the gray forest below shivered and the mist one minute enveloped the shapes of the mountains and the next half disclosed their powerful reaches; it oppressed him, he was searching for something, as though for lost dreams, but he found nothing. Everything was so small to him, so close, so damp; he'd have liked to set the earth behind the stove to dry. He couldn't understand why it required so much time to descend a slope and reach a distant point; he thought he should be able to arrive there in a couple of steps. Sometimes the storm hurled clouds into the valleys and they swept through the forest, and voices awakened on the rocky slopes, one moment like distant echoing thunder and the next like a powerful surge that sounded as though in its uncontrolled jubilation it wanted to celebrate the earth. The clouds, like wild, neighing horses, sprang forward, and the sun shone through them and penetrated the snowfields with its glittering sword, so that a bright, blinding light cut its way down from the summits into the valleys. Or sometimes the storm drove the clouds downwards, tearing them apart to reveal a light blue lake, and then the wind echoed and, from the depths of the gorge, from the tops of the pines, hummed its way up like a cradle song and the chiming of bells. A faint crimson ascended the deep blue of the sky and tiny clouds on silver wings sailed through it, and all the mountain peaks, strong and stable, glittered and sparkled across the landscape. All this tore into his breast; he stood there, gasping for breath, his body bent forwards, eyes and mouth wide open. He felt as if he must pull the storm inside himself, contain all things in himself; he stretched himself out and lay across the earth, he burrowed himself into the universe, as though it were a joy that caused him pain; or else he stopped and laid his head in the moss and half closed his eyes, and then it all went far away from him, the earth sunk from under him, it grew small as a wandering star and dipped into a raging storm whose clear waters swept beneath him. But these were only moments; then he rose, clear-headed, strong, calm, as though a shadow-play had passed before him—he knew nothing of what had happened.

Toward evening he arrived at the summit of the mountain, the snowfield, from which one began to make one's way down again toward the plains in the west. He sat down, there on the summit. It had grown more peaceful toward evening; the clouds hung firm and unmoving in the sky; as far as the eye could see there were mountain peaks with broad slopes leading down from them, and everything was so still, gray, and dusky. He became terribly lonely; he was alone, all alone. He wanted to talk with himself, but he couldn't, he scarcely dared breathe; the bending of his feet cracked like thunder beneath him, he had to sit down. He was gripped by a nameless fear in this nothingness: he was in a void! He rose quickly and rushed down the slope.

Darkness had come on, heaven and earth melted into one. It was as if he were being followed, as if something horrible would overtake him, something which no man could endure, as if madness were chasing behind him with its horses.

At last he heard voices; he saw some lights, he felt relieved. They told him he had still a half hour before reaching Waldbach.

He went through the village. Lights shone through the windows, he looked in while passing: children sitting at the table, old women, girls, their faces calm and serene. It seemed to him the light streamed from these faces. He felt better, he was almost at the parsonage in Waldbach.

They sat around the table, he was with them; his blond curls hung down around his pale face, his eyes and mouth twitched, his clothes were torn.

Oberlin welcomed him, he took him for an artisan:

"You are welcome in this house, even though I do not know you."

"I am a friend of Kaufmann's; he asked me to give you his greeting."

"May I know your name?"

"Lenz."

"Why, yes, yes, haven't I seen it in print? Haven't I read some plays by a gentleman of that name?"

"Yes, but you mustn't judge me by that."

They continued talking; he searched for words and spoke rapidly, but he was in torment. After a while he grew quiet—there in the comfortable room with those calm faces that stood out in the shadows: the bright face of a child, upon which all light seemed to rest, and which looked up questioningly and trustingly, and then her mother sitting back there in the shadow, so like an angel. He began to tell them about his home; he drew all kinds of costumes, they gathered around him with interest, he at once felt at home. His pale child's face was smiling now, and his talk was lively. He grew peaceful; it seemed as if old figures with forgotten faces reappeared to him from the dark past, old songs reawakened: he was far, far away.

Finally it was time to leave. Because the parsonage was too small, they took him across the road and gave him a room in the schoolhouse. He went upstairs. It was cold up there; a wide room that was empty, with a high bed in the background. He placed the lamp on the table and paced back and forth. He thought again about the day just past, how he had come here, where he was. The room in the parsonage with its lights and dear faces seemed like a shadow now, like a dream, and he felt empty again, as on the mountain; but he could not fill this emptiness with anything. The light was out, darkness swallowed up all things. He felt gripped by an unnamable fear. He leapt from bed, ran down the stairs to the front of the house; but all in vain, everything was dark, nothing—he himself was a dream. Isolated thoughts rushed through his mind; he held fast to them. It seemed he should be always repeating the "Lord's Prayer." He was lost; an obscure instinct drove him to save himself. He thrust himself against the stones, he tore himself with his nails; the pain began, bringing him to his senses. He threw himself into the fountain, but the water wasn't deep, he splashed about.

People began to gather; they had heard the noise and called to him. Oberlin came running. Lenz had come to himself, he was wholly conscious of the situation, he felt relieved. He felt ashamed now and distressed that he had caused these kind people so much anxiety. He told them he was accustomed to bathing in cold water, and went back to his room. His exhaustion allowed him some repose.

The next morning everything went well. He and Oberlin rode through the valley on horseback; wide mountain slopes which at a great height shrank into a narrow, winding valley, which twisted its way to the heights in many directions; great masses of stone that grew broad at their bases; a few trees, but everything with a gray, somber tinge; a view towards the west across the countryside and the mountain chain that ran in a north-south direction, whose peaks towered there in quiet, earnest strength, as though in a twilit dream. At times intense masses of light rose from the valley like a flood of gold; then clouds again, which lay on the topmost peaks, and then slowly descended into the valley through the forest, or else rose and sank in the sun's rays like a flying, silver ghost; no sound, no movement, no birds, nothing but the now near, now far, sighing of the wind. There also appeared the skeletons of huts, boards covered with straw, dark and gloomy. The people, silent and grave, greeted them quietly as they rode past, as though they dared not disturb the peace of their valley.

There was a liveliness inside the huts; they thronged around Oberlin; he admonished them, counseled them, consoled them; their eyes were full of trust, they prayed. The people told of their dreams, their premonitions. Then suddenly back again to the matters of practical life: the laying of new roads, the digging of canals, a visit to the school.

Oberlin was untiring, and Lenz his constant companion, sometimes in conversation, sometimes busied with manual labor, sometimes lost in Nature. This life had a salutary effect and calmed him. He often looked into Oberlin's eyes, and in those quiet eyes, in this noble, serious face, he saw that immense peace which overtakes us in the repose of Nature, in the depths of the forest, on melting, moonlit summer nights—all this seemed even closer to him in this man's countenance. Lenz was shy; but he commented on things, he spoke. Oberlin enjoyed his conversation, and the pleasant childlike face of Lenz gave him great pleasure.

But only as long as there was light in the valley were things bearable to Lenz; as evening came on he was overcome by a strange anxiety, he felt he wanted to run after the sun. As his surroundings grew darker in shadow, everything seemed dreamlike to him, repugnant; anxiety took hold of him like a child who must sleep in the dark; he felt as if he were blind. And now it grew, this mountain of madness shot up at his feet; the hopeless thought that everything was a dream spread itself out in front of him; he clung to all solid objects. Figures rapidly passed him by, he pressed toward them; they were shadows, life withdrew from him, his limbs were numb. He spoke, he sang, he recited passages from Shakespeare, he grasped at everything that might make his blood flow faster, he tried everything, but—he was cold, cold! Then he had to go out into the open. When his eyes became used to the darkness, the faint glow that dispersed itself through the night comforted him. He thrust himself into the spring; the harsh effect of the water comforted him. He also harbored a secret hope that it would make him ill—when he bathed now, he did so with less commotion.

Yet the more accustomed he grew to the life around him, the more composed he became. He was a help to Oberlin, he drew, he read the Bible. Old hopes of the past reawakened in him. The New Testament was especially brought home to him here. Oberlin had told him that once an invisible hand had grasped him on the bridge, that on the summits a dazzling light had once blinded him, that he had heard a voice, that it had spoken with him in the night, and that God had so much entered into him that like a child he took his fate into his hands in order to know what he must do. This faith, this eternal Heaven on earth, this living in God, revealed the Holy Scriptures to him for the first time. How close Nature came to these people, all things were holy mysteries; but not with overpowering majesty, rather with simple intimacy.

One morning he went out. Snow had fallen that night; the valley was flooded with bright sunshine, but farther on the landscape lay half in mist. He soon left the path and ascended a gentle slope beside a pine forest; there was no trace of footprints any more. The sun made crystal of the snow, which was light and fluffy; here and there the track of game was lightly imprinted on the snow as it made its way into the mountains. No movement in the air except for the soft sighing of the wind, or the rustle of a bird lightly dusting snowflakes from his tail. Nothing but silence, and the trees in the distance with white, waving branches against the deep blue of the sky. He began to feel comfortable after a while. The vast, monotonous expanses, and the contours of the mountains, which at times seemed to speak to him in powerful tones, were hidden. A comfortable feeling, as of Christmas, crept over him; he thought at times that his mother would appear, grandly, from behind a tree, and say to him that she had given him all this as a gift. As he descended he saw that a rainbow of rays lay around his shadow; it

seemed as if something had touched him on the forehead, as if that something spoke to him.

He came down the mountain. Oberlin was in his room;
Lenz approached him happily and said that he would like
to preach for once.

"Are you a student of theology?"

"Yes!"

"Very well, then, next Sunday."

Lenz went to his room pleased. He thought of a text
for his sermon and lost himself in contemplation, and his
nights became quiet. The Sunday morning came, a thaw
had set in. Clouds floated past with flecks of blue in
them. The church lay beside the mountain on a promi-
nence, the churchyard behind it. Lenz stood high up as
the bells rang out and watched the congregation coming
from all directions rise and descend with the narrow path
that wound between the rocks; women and girls in their
somber black dresses, with a white folded handkerchief
and a sprig of rosemary on their hymnbooks. A bright
ray of sunshine occasionally filled the valley, the mild air
moved gently. The countryside was bathed in a fragrance,
bells pealed in the distance—it seemed as if all things
had dissolved into a wave of harmony.

The snow was gone from the little churchyard; dark
moss grew beneath the black crosses. A late rosebush
bloomed at the churchyard wall, and late flowers grew
up among the moss. At times there was sun, then shadow
again. The church service began, the voices of the people
united in pure, bright sounds; it gave the impression of
looking into a clear, transparent mountain stream. The
hymn died away—Lenz spoke. He was shy. During the
singing his numbness had completely disappeared; his
sense of suffering wakened now and took its place in his
heart. A sweet feeling of endless well-being came over
him. He spoke to the people with simple words; they
were all his fellow sufferers, and it was a consolation to
him if he could bring peace to eyes tired from crying
and to troubled souls, if he could lead to Heaven these
beings tormented with material needs and heavy sorrow.
He felt stronger and he concluded—then the singing
began again:

Let my soul give rise to fountains,
Rent in me through blessèd pain;
Suffering be my sacred service,
Suffering be all my gain.

The pressure inside him, the music, the suffering, shat
tered him. For him the universe was an open wound; i
caused him deep, inexplicable pain. But now a new be
ing opened itself to him: a divine, tremulous mouth ben
down above him and drew him to its lips; he went t
his solitary room. He was alone, alone! A spring of emo
tion rushed from him, his eyes broke into streams, h
was convulsed, his limbs twitched, it seemed as if h
would dissolve, this ecstasy would never end. Finally i
died away: he sensed a quiet, deep pity for himself, h
cried over himself; his head sank onto his breast, he wa
asleep. The full moon hung in the Heavens; the locks o
his hair fell across his temples and his face, tears hun
on his eyelashes and dried on his cheeks—so he lay ther
alone, and all was quiet and still and cold, and the moo
shone the whole night and hung there above the moun
tains.

On the following morning he came down and explaine
to Oberlin quite calmly how during the night his moth
had appeared to him. She had stepped forth from th
dark churchyard wall in a white dress, with a white ros
and a red rose at her breast; she sank down in a corne
then and the roses slowly grew over her; she was surel
dead. He was quite calm. Oberlin had told him how a
the time of his father's death he was alone in the field
and then heard a voice which told him his father wa
dead; and upon arriving home, he found it to be so. Thi
led them on: Oberlin told of the people in the moun
tains, of girls who divined water and metal under th
earth, and of men who were seized on mountaintops an
wrestled with a spirit. He told him too that once in th
mountains he had been thrown into a sort of trance a
a result of looking into a deep, empty mountain poo
Lenz said that the spirit of the waters had come over him
too, and that it was then that he had discovered thing
about his own being. He continued. He said that th
simplest, purest people were those who were near th

elemental; that the more refined a man's feelings and
life, the more blunted this elemental sense becomes. He
did not consider this a very high form of being, it wasn't
self-sufficient enough; but he thought that it must be
a feeling of endless bliss to be in such close contact with
the particular life of every form, to have a soul for rocks,
metals, water, and plants, to take into himself, as in a
dream, every element of Nature, like flowers that breathe
with the waxing and waning of the moon.

He expressed himself further. He said that each thing
possessed its own inexpressible harmony, its own sound,
its own blessedness; that higher forms with more organs
were able better to choose, to express, to understand, and
were therefore more deeply affected; and that lower
forms were more repressed, more restricted, and therefore
enjoyed a greater degree of tranquillity. He pursued his
line of thought further, but Oberlin put an end to it
because it led him too far afield from his simple ideas.
Another time he showed Lenz some color charts and ex-
plained to him the correspondence between color and each
type of human being. He showed him the Twelve Apostles
and how each was represented by his own particular color.
Lenz took all this in, developed the ideas still further,
suffered from uneasy dreams, and, like Jung-Stilling, began
reading the Apocalypse, and read widely in the Bible.

Around this time Kaufmann and his wife came to
Steintal. At first Lenz was displeased with having to meet
him; he had just arranged this comfortable place for
himself, his measure of tranquillity was so precious to
him—and now there came someone who reminded him
of so many things, whom he had to talk to and converse
with, someone who knew the circumstances of his life.
Oberlin knew nothing of all this; he had taken him in,
cared for him. Lenz saw in it the finger of God, that he,
miserable, was sent to this man; he loved Oberlin dearly.
And it was necessary to all concerned that he should stay
there; he belonged to them as though he had been there
for a long while, and no one asked where he had come
from and whither he would go.

At table Lenz was again in good spirits. They spoke of
literature, he was in his proper sphere. The period of

Idealism was then in fashion, and Kaufmann was its disciple. Lenz spoke violently against it. He said that those poets who claimed to represent reality hadn't even conception of it; nonetheless they are more bearable than those who want to glorify reality. He said that the good Lord had indeed made the world as it should be and we ought not think ourselves capable of improving upon it our sole endeavor should be to imitate Him a bit.

"I demand of art that it be life and the possibility that it might exist—nothing else matters; we then have no need to ask whether it is beautiful or ugly. The sense that what has been created has life stands above the other two precepts and is the only criterion of art. Furthermore, we find it only very seldom: we find it in Shakespeare, we are always confronted with it in folk songs, and sometimes in Goethe; whatever else there is we can toss out as worthless. These people can't so much as draw a dog's kennel. They try to create ideal forms, but all that I have seen of their work looks more like wooden dolls. Idealism is the most humiliating of insults to human nature. Let them try just once to immerse themselves in the life of humble people and then reproduce this again in all its movements, its implications, in its subtle, scarcely discernible play of expression; I attempted just that in my plays The Tutor and The Soldiers. They contain the most prosaic characters under the sun; but the organs of feeling are the same in almost all men; the only difference is the thickness of the crust through which it must break. One must have an eye and ear for such things. As I walked in the valley yesterday I saw two girls sitting on a rock one of them was binding up her hair, and the other helped her with it. Her golden hair hung down, her face serious and pale and so young, her dress was black, and the other girl so attentive to help her. The finest, most sincere paintings of the Old German School scarcely give an impression of such a scene. One might wish at times to be a Medusa's head, so as to be able to transform such a group into stone and summon the world to see it. Then they rose, and the beautiful grouping was destroyed but as they descended between the rocks they formed another picture.

"The most beautiful pictures, the most swelling tones, form a group and then dissolve. Only one thing remains: an unending beauty which passes from one form to another, eternally revealed, eternally unchanged. Of course we can't always hold them fast and place them in museums and reduce them to manuscript paper, and then lead the young and old there to see them and lecture to boys and old men about them and let them go into ecstasies. One must love mankind in order to penetrate the particular existence of each thing; there must be nothing too common, or too ugly. Only then can they be understood. The most insignificant of faces can make a deeper impression than the mere sensation of beauty. One can create forms and let them emanate from him without copying anything of Nature, forms in which there is neither life, nor muscle, nor the throbbing pulsation of the blood."

Kaufmann reproached him with saying that nowhere in reality would he find a type equal to the Apollo Belvedere or a Raphael Madonna.

"What does that matter?" rejoined Lenz. "I must confess that these works leave me rather dead. If I worked at it I might be able to arouse an interest in myself in regard to them; but I'm the one who does most of the work. Those poets and painters are my favorites who represent Nature to me as she really is, so that I can feel something in regard to the work. Everything else disturbs me. I prefer the Dutch painters over the Italians; they are also the only ones capable of being understood. I know of only two paintings, and both of them by Dutch painters, which make an impression on me like that I receive from the New Testament. One of them is that of Christ and the Disciples from Emmaus. I don't recall the painter. When one reads in the New Testament how the Disciples went out, one finds all of Nature in those few words. It is a gloomy evening at twilight, a monotonous line of crimson on the horizon, the road half dark. Suddenly a stranger comes toward them, they talk, he breaks bread with them. Then they recognize Him in His simple human form, and the divine suffering face reveals itself to them, and they are afraid, because it has grown dark, and they are met with a mystery. But it is not the

terror of seeing a ghost; it is as if at twilight one were
meeting someone now dead, whom one had loved, and
he looked as he used to look. That's how the painting is,
with its monotonous brown tone and the quiet gloomy
evening. Then there's another painting. A woman sitting
in her chamber with her prayerbook in her hand. The
house has been cleaned in preparation for Sunday, sand
strewn on the floor, comfortably clean and warm. The
woman has been unable to go to church, and she is per-
forming her devotions at home. The window is open,
and she sits facing it, and it is as if the sounds of bells
from the village floated in at her window across the wide,
flat landscape, and the singing of the nearby congregation
echoed from the church, and the woman reads her text
after them."

He continued speaking in this manner; they listened
to him, and many others joined them. He had grown
flushed with speaking, smiling one moment, and the next
shaking his blond locks. He had completely forgotten himself.

After the meal Kaufmann took him aside. He had
received letters from Lenz's father saying that his son
should come back and be a support to him. Kaufmann
told him that he was throwing away his life here, wasting
it unnecessarily, that he should find a goal for himself,
and so on.

Lenz let fly at him: "Leave here? Go away? Go home?
And go mad there? You know that I can live nowhere
else but here, in this region. If I couldn't sometimes
climb a mountain and see the countryside, and then come
back here to the house, walk through the gardens, look
in at the window—I would go mad! Leave me in peace!
Just a little peace, now that it begins to do me some
good! Leave? Leave? I don't understand. Those few
words spoil the world for me. Everyone has something
that he needs; but when a man can rest, what more can
he need? Always striving, struggling, and eternally throwing away what the moment offers and always starving oneself so as eventually to enjoy something! To be dying of
thirst while a clear spring bounds across your path! I can
endure my life now. I'll stay here. Why? Why? Because

I feel well here. What does my father want? Can he offer me more than that? Impossible! Leave me in peace!"

He grew violent. Kaufmann left him. Lenz was disturbed.

The next day Kaufmann wanted to leave. He persuaded Oberlin to go to Switzerland with him. The desire to get to know Lavater personally, whom he had for a long while known only through letters, decided him. He agreed to go. But they would have to wait an extra day to prepare themselves for the journey. Lenz was deeply struck by this. In order to rid himself of his unending torment he anxiously grasped onto everything; at isolated moments he felt deeply how he was making excuses for everything; he treated himself as though he were a child who was sick. He was able to rid himself of many thoughts and overpowering emotions only as the result of great anguish; then they only returned to oppress him with boundless violence. He trembled, his hair almost stood on end, until he had exhausted himself through the most terrible strain. He was able to save himself through one image which was always in his sight, and through Oberlin; his words, his face, did him an endless amount of good. And so he thought of Oberlin's journey with anxiety.

Lenz felt uneasy at being left alone in the house. The weather had become mild; he decided to accompany Oberlin into the mountains. On the other side, where the valley spread into the plain, they parted. He walked back alone. He roamed through the mountains in various directions. The wide slopes made their way down to the valleys, there was little forest, only the powerful contour of the rocks, and farther out the broad, smoking plain.

There was a mighty sighing in the air, nowhere any sign of a human being, except for an occasional deserted hut resting on a slope where the shepherds spent their summer. He grew quiet, perhaps almost lost in a dream; everything melted into a single line, like a wave rising and falling between Heaven and earth. It seemed to him he lay in an infinite sea that gently rose and fell. At times he seated himself; then continued on, slowly, dreaming. He sought out no way in particular.

The evening was dark when he arrived at an inhabited

hut on a slope beyond Steintal. The door was locked. He went to the window through which came a beam of light. A lamp lighted only a portion of the room; its light fell on the pale features of a girl resting in the background; her eyes half open, her lips moving gently. Farther back in the darkness sat an old woman who sang from a hymn-book in a rasping voice. After long knocking she opened the door; she was half deaf. She brought Lenz some food and showed him a place to sleep, at the same time continuing her singing. The girl had not moved. After a while a man came in; he was tall and haggard, traces of gray hair, and a restless, confused face. He went to the girl, her body twitched and grew restless. He took a dried herb from the wall and placed the leaves on her hands so that she became calmer and began to murmur distinct words in a slow, piercing voice. The man told him how he had heard a voice in the mountains and then seen summer lightning over the valleys; and something had seized him, too, and he wrestled with it like Jacob with the Angel. He threw himself down and prayed softly and with fervor, while the sick girl sang in a long-drawn-out voice that softly faded away. Then he went to bed.

Lenz went to sleep dreaming, and in his sleep he heard the ticking of the clock. The soughing of the wind, near now, and then distant, was heard through the girl's soft singing and the voices of the old couple; the moon cast a shifting, dreamlike light into the room as clouds drifted across its surface. Once the sounds grew louder, the girl spoke distinctly and clearly; she said that a church stood on the rock opposite. Lenz looked up and saw her sitting at the table with eyes wide open, and the moon cast its still light on her features which seemed to radiate an uncanny light. Finally, amidst the rasping of the old woman, the coming and going of the moon's shifting light, and the other sounds and voices, Lenz fell into a deep sleep.

He woke early. The others were asleep in the dimly lit room, including the girl, who had grown peaceful. She lay leaned back, her hands folded under her left cheek; the ghostly look had left her features, she wore an expression of indescribable suffering. He walked to the win-

dow and opened it, the cold morning air struck his face.
The house lay at the end of a deep, narrow valley that
opened toward the east. Crimson rays shot through the
gray morning sky into the half-light of the valley, which
lay in white mist. The sun's rays sparkled on the gray
rocks and shone through the windows of the huts. The
man awoke. His eyes rested on an illuminated picture on
the wall, they stared at it hard and fixedly. His lips began
to move and he prayed softly, growing louder and louder.
At the same time others came into the hut and threw
themselves down silently. The girl lay there in convulsions,
the old woman rasped out her song and spoke with her
neighbors.

These people told Lenz that the man had come to the
region years ago from no one knows where. He had the
reputation of being a saint; he could divine water under
the earth, could conjure up spirits, and people made pil-
grimages to him. Lenz learned at the same time that
he was quite a distance from Steintal; so he left with some
woodcutters going in that direction. It did him good to be
in company; he felt uncomfortable with that powerful
man who at times it seemed to him spoke in a terrible
voice. He was also afraid of himself when he was alone.

He came home. The past night had made a powerful
impression on him. The world was a bright place to him,
yet he sensed a stirring and turmoil inside him that tore
him in the direction of an abyss with unrelenting violence. He felt a gnawing inside himself. He ate little. Half
the night he sat up praying and in feverish dreams. He
felt a violent pressure and then he collapsed in exhaustion;
he lay in scalding hot tears. Then suddenly he regained
his strength and rose up cold and indifferent; his tears
were like ice then; it made him laugh. The higher he
forced himself to climb, the farther he had to fall. Everything seemed to stream together. Recollections of his
earlier life suddenly flashed through him and cast blinding lights on the wild chaos of his mind.

During the day he generally sat in the room downstairs.
Frau Oberlin went in and out. He drew, painted, read,
grasped at any distractions, hurrying from one thing to
the next. He especially attached himself now to Frau

Oberlin when she sat there, her black hymnbook in front of her, beside one of her domestic plants, her youngest child between her knees. He also often occupied himself with the children. He was sitting there that way once when he grew frightened; he jumped up and walked back and forth. The door half open, he heard the maid's singing outside; not understandable at first, he finally caught the words:

> *This world it has no joy for me,*
> *I have my love, but where is he?*

He was so struck by this that he almost fainted. Frau Oberlin looked at him. He summoned courage; he could no longer remain silent; he had to speak of it.

"My dearest Frau Oberlin, could you tell me perhaps what has happened to the woman whose fate hangs upon me like lead?"

"Why, I know nothing about it, Herr Lenz."

He was silent again and walked back and forth in the room; then he began again:

"I'm sorry, but I must leave here. God only knows you are the only people I can endure living with, and yet—and yet, I must go, to her—but I can't, I don't dare." He was deeply distressed and left the room.

Toward evening Lenz returned; the room was growing dark. He sat down beside Frau Oberlin.

"You see," he began again, "when she simply walked through the room, singing half to herself, and every step of hers was music, there was a kind of happiness in her that overflowed into me. I was always at peace when I saw her or leaned her head against me like this.—She was just a child; it was as if the world were too wide for her. She shrank so into herself; she would always seek out the narrowest places in the entire house, and sit there as though all her happiness were drawn together into that small place, and then it became that way for me. I could have played like a child. And now everything has become so narrow, so narrow! At times it is as if I were pounding with my hands at the top of Heaven. Oh, I'm suffocating! It often happens that I sense a physical pain, here in my left side, in this arm with which I once clasped her. Yet now I can picture her no longer, her image escapes me, and the thought of it tortures me. Only at those times when I can see her clearly do I feel as if I am well."

Later he oftentimes spoke of the girl to Frau Oberlin, but generally in disjointed sentences. She didn't know how to answer, but it did him good all the same.

In the meanwhile his religious torments continued. The emptier, the colder, the more dead he felt in himself, just that much more did he feel the urgency to wake a sense of life within him. He recalled the times when everything inside him oppressed him, when he became exhausted by every sensation. And now to be so dead. He despaired of himself, then threw himself down, wrung his hands, stirred up everything inside himself—but he was dead! Dead! Then he implored God to send him a sign; then he probed in himself, fasted, and lay dreaming on the floor.

On the third of February he heard that in Fouday a girl named Friederike had died. It became an obsession with him. He retired to his room and fasted an entire day. On the fourth he suddenly entered the room and faced Frau Oberlin. He had smeared his face with ashes and he asked for an old sack. She was frightened, but gave him what he wanted. He wrapped the sack around him like a penitent and took the road to Fouday. The people in the valley were already accustomed to him; they told one another all sorts of strange things about him. He entered the house where the child lay. The people went about their business; they directed him to a room; the child lay in its nightshirt on a table, in a bed of straw.

Lenz shuddered as he touched the cold limbs and saw the half-opened glassy eyes. The child seemed so forsaken, and he himself so alone, so solitary. He threw himself down across the body. Death frightened him; an overwhelming grief gripped him. These features, this silent face, had to molder in the earth. He prayed in all the misery of despair that God show him a sign that he might return the child to life. He then turned wholly into himself and summoned all his will to a single point. He sat there stiffly for a long while. Then he rose, took the child's hands in his own and spoke in a loud, firm voice: "Arise and walk!" But the walls echoed his words back emptily, as if in mockery, and the body remained cold. He fell down, half mad; then it chased him to his feet again and out into the mountains.

Clouds swept rapidly across the moon; one moment everything lay in darkness, and the next the countryside lay revealed, half hidden by mist, in the moonlight. He ran one way then another. A hellish song of triumph sang inside him. The wind resounded like a song of Titans. He felt as if he could raise a monstrous fist to the Heavens and tear God down and drag Him through His clouds; as if he could grind the world together with his teeth and spit it out into the Creator's face. He cursed, he blasphemed. And so he arrived at the summit of the mountain. The uncertain light made its way down to where the white masses of stone lay, and the sky was a stupid blue eye from which the moon looked out laughably, stupidly. Lenz laughed loudly, and with that laugh atheism took hold of him surely and calmly and firmly. He no longer knew what had disturbed him so before; it made him freeze. He thought then that he wanted to go to bed, and he walked cold and unshakably through the gloomy dark. Everything was empty and hollow. He had to run, and went to bed.

The following day he awoke horrified by his state on the previous day. He stood now at an abyss, and derived a mad delight from looking down into it and reliving his torment. Then his terror increased; he was faced with his sin against the Holy Ghost.

A few days later Oberlin returned from Switzerland, considerably sooner than anticipated. Lenz was taken by surprise. But he was pleased when Oberlin told him of his friends in Alsace. While doing so he walked back and forth in his room, unpacking, and putting his things away. He told him about Pfeffel, happily praising the life of a country pastor. Thereupon he admonished Lenz to follow his father's wishes, to live according to his calling and return home. He said to him: "Honor your father and your mother!" and so on. Their conversation unsettled Lenz considerably; he sighed deeply, tears forced their way from his eyes, he spoke disjointedly.

"I can't bear it; are you trying to get rid of me? My only way to God is through you. As for me, there is nothing left! I've sinned, I'm damned for eternity, I am the Wandering Jew."

Oberlin told him that was why Jesus died; he must turn ardently to Him, and he would share in His grace.

Lenz raised his head, wrung his hands, and said: "My God, my God! Divine consolation——" Then he asked suddenly in a friendly way what he had heard of the lady. Oberlin replied that he knew nothing, but that he wanted to help and advise him in everything; he must tell him the place, the conditions, and the person concerned.

Lenz answered only in disjointed sentences: "Is she dead? Is she still alive? She was an angel! She loved me—I loved her, as she had to be loved—the angel! Damnable jealousy! I sacrificed her—she loved someone else—I loved her as she had to be loved—and my dear mother, she loved me, too—I've murdered you both!"

Oberlin replied that perhaps these people were still alive, and happy; but be it as it might be, God could and would favor his prayers and tears if he returned to Him; God would show them so much good that perhaps the benefits they might have had from him, and the harm that he once did them, might be outweighed by that goodness of God. He slowly became calmer and more assured and went back to his painting.

That afternoon he returned. On his left shoulder he had a piece of fur and in his hand a bundle of sapling branches which someone had given Oberlin together with a letter for Lenz. He handed Oberlin the branches, kissed him several times on the mouth and said that these were the stripes he had to give him. He was told to be calm and settle his affairs alone with God, because all the stripes in the world could not expiate a single sin. Jesus would take care of that, therefore he must turn to Him. He went away.

At supper he was pensive as usual. Yet he spoke of all sorts of things, but with hasty anxiety. At about midnight

Oberlin was wakened by a noise. Lenz ran through the courtyard and in a hollow, harsh voice cried out the name of Friederike with extreme rapidity, confusion, and despair. He then threw himself into the basin of the fountain, splashed about, ran up again to his room, then down again and into the basin, and so on a number of times—finally he was quiet. The maids who slept in the nursery below him said that they had often heard a kind of humming, and that night especially, which reminded them of the wail of a ghost. Perhaps it was his moaning in a hollow, frightened, despairing voice.

The following day Lenz remained in his room longer than usual. Finally Oberlin went up to see him; he lay in bed, quiet and unmoving. Oberlin had to question him a long while before receiving an answer; finally he said:

"Yes, Pastor Oberlin, it's boredom! Oh, this boredom! I scarcely know any more what to say; I've drawn all kinds of figures on the walls."

Oberlin told him to turn to God; this made Lenz laugh and say:

"How I wish I were as fortunate as you to have so comfortable a pastime. One could very easily spend his time that way. Everything for idleness' sake. After all, most people pray out of boredom, others fall in love out of boredom, some are virtuous, some vicious, and I am nothing, absolutely nothing! I don't even want to take my own life: it would be too boring!

> O God within your waves of light,
> In your noonday glowing bright,
> My eyes with watching now are sore;
> Will night never soothe me more?

Oberlin looked at him with vexation and was about to leave. Lenz rushed after him and, looking at him with uncanny eyes, said:

"An idea's come to me after all; I wish I could decide whether I was dreaming or waking. That's very important, you see; we must look into the matter," and rushed back to his bed.

That afternoon Oberlin intended to pay a visit in the neighborhood; his wife was already gone. He was on the

point of leaving, when there came a knocking at the door
and Lenz entered with his body bent forward, his head
hung down, his face smeared all over with ashes and his
clothes smeared here and there; he held his left arm with
his right hand. He asked Oberlin to pull on his arm; he
had dislocated it when he fell from his window. Since no
one had seen it, he wanted to say nothing about it.
Oberlin was greatly startled, though he said nothing; he
did as Lenz asked him. At the same time he wrote to the
schoolmaster Sebastian Scheidecker at Bellefosse to come
and tell him what to do. Then he rode off.

The man came. Lenz had seen him often and grown
attached to him. He acted as though he wanted to speak
to Oberlin about a matter, and then was about to leave.
Lenz asked him to stay, and so they stayed there together.
Lenz suggested another walk to Fouday. He visited the
grave of the child he had wanted to bring to life, knelt
down in front of various pictures, kissed the mound of the
grave, seemed to pray, though in great confusion, tore
something from the wreath on the grave as a memento,
went back to Waldbach, and then returned once more, the
schoolmaster with him. At times he walked slowly, complaining of a weakness in his limbs, and at other times
walked with desperate speed. He was frightened of the
countryside; it was so narrow that he was afraid of bump-
ing into everything. An indescribable feeling of displeasure
came over him; his companion he found oppressive; also,
perhaps, he had realized his reason for being there and
therefore sought means of getting rid of him. Sebastian
appeared to give in to him, but found devious means of
informing his brother of the danger, and so Lenz had two
keepers instead of one. He gave them a thorough leading
around, then finally turned back to Waldbach; as they
came near the village he turned about like lightning and
like a stag bolted back toward Fouday. The men followed
him. While looking for him in Fouday they ran into two
tradesmen who told them that there was a stranger tied up
in one of the houses, who gave himself out to be a
murderer, but who obviously was nothing of the kind.
They ran to the house and saw it was so. A young man
had tied up Lenz at his own violent insistence. They un-

bound him and peacefully led him back to Waldbach, whither Oberlin and his wife had already returned. He appeared confused. But when he perceived that he was welcomed back with love and friendship he took courage again; his face changed to its former self and he thanked his companions in a friendly and tender way, and that evening took a quiet walk. Oberlin urged him not to bathe any more, and to stay quietly in bed at night; if unable to sleep, then he should converse with God. He promised and did so the following night. The maids below heard him praying almost the entire night.

The next morning he went to Oberlin's room seeming very pleased. After they had spoken of various matters, Lenz said with uncommon friendliness:

"My dear Pastor Oberlin, the lady about whom I spoke to you has died, yes, she has died—that angel!"

"Who told you that?"

"Hieroglyphics, from hieroglyphics!" Then he looked up at the Heavens and said again: "Yes, she's dead— hieroglyphics!" After that he would say no more. He sat down and wrote several letters, then handed them to Oberlin with the request that he add a few sentences.

Meanwhile his condition grew more and more disconsolate. All the tranquillity that he had derived from Oberlin's presence and from the quietness of the valley had left him. The world he had once hoped to serve was severed by a monstrous gap; he had neither hatred, nor love, nor hope—only a dreadful void in himself, and a tremendous restlessness to fill it. He had nothing. What he did, he did with no consciousness, and yet he was driven by an inner impulse. When alone, he was so dreadfully lonely that he constantly spoke out loud with himself, called out, and then grew startled as though a strange voice had spoken with him. He often stammered in conversation; an indescribable fear came over him that he had forgotten the end of his sentence; then he thought that he must hold fast to the last word spoken and continue speaking; he suppressed this desire only with intense effort. He troubled the good people deeply when during some quiet moment while sitting among them, talking calmly, he would begin to stammer and an indescribable fear would come into his face; then he would convulsively grasp hold of the arm of the person next to him and only after a while come to himself. If he was alone, or reading, it was even worse; at times his entire mental faculties would become obsessed with a single idea. If he thought of another person, or tried to imagine him, then it seemed he became that person. He grew completely confused and at times was driven by a deep impulse to associate despotically, at least in his mind, with everything around him—Nature, Man; only Oberlin was excluded. He amused himself by standing houses on their roofs, by mentally dressing and undressing people, and by thinking up absurd practical jokes. At times he sensed an irresistible urge to carry through what he had devised in his mind, and that caused him to grimace terribly. Once he sat next to Oberlin and saw the cat lying opposite them on the chair. Suddenly Lenz's eyes became fixed, he held them steadily on the animal. Then slowly he slid from his chair, the cat moved with him; she seemed hypnotized by his look, she became terrified, her fur bristled. Lenz responded in the same way, his face horribly distorted; then as if in despair they flung themselves at one another. Finally Frau Oberlin rose to part them. That made him deeply ashamed again. The incidents of his nights rose to a terrible pitch. It was only with the most intense effort that he fell asleep, and then only after trying to fill the void inside him. He then fell into a terrible state between waking and sleeping; he collided with something terrible, something horrible, and was seized with madness. Bathed in sweat, he flung himself from his bed with a blood-curdling scream, and only found himself after a while. In order to keep hold on himself he had to occupy himself with the simplest of things. In reality it wasn't he who did them, but a powerful sense of self-preservation. It was as if he were two entities, and one entity tried to save the other and called across to himself. He was told that when at his worst he would recite poetry until he had control of himself again.

He even had these attacks during the day, and then they were even more terrible, because till now the daylight had protected him. At times like this it seemed as if he existed all alone, as if the world had its only place in his imagination, as if there were nothing but himself; he believed himself eternally damned, Satan, alone with his tormenting thoughts. He ran through the events of his life with insane speed and then said: "It follows, it follows"; and when someone else said something he replied: "That doesn't follow, that doesn't follow." It was the abyss of incurable madness, a madness that would last for eternity.

The urge of self-preservation chased him from his bed; he thrust himself into Oberlin's arms, he clung to the man as though he wanted to become one with him; he was the only being who had any existence for him, and through whom he hoped to have life revealed to him again. Gradually Oberlin's words would bring him to himself again; he would fall on his knees in front of Oberlin, his hands in Oberlin's, his face drenched in cold sweat on Oberlin's lap, his whole body trembling and shaking. Oberlin was capable of infinite pity; his family fell to its knees and prayed for the unfortunate man; the maids fled from him and regarded him as one possessed. When he grew calmer his misery was like that of a child: he sobbed, he felt a deep, deep pity for himself. These were his happiest moments. Oberlin spoke to him of God. Lenz quietly wrenched himself loose and looked at him with an expression of boundless pity, and said:

"Yes, you see, if I were almighty, if I were that, I could not endure this suffering; I would save Man from it, save him. All I ask is rest, rest, just a little rest, so that I can sleep."

Oberlin said this was a profanation. Lenz shook his head hopelessly.

Meanwhile he made several attempts at suicide, none of them very much in earnest. They were less the will to die—since there was for him neither peace nor hope in death—than they were attempts to gain control of himself at moments of the most intense fear or at times of apathetic peace that bordered on nonbeing. Moments in which his mind seemed wholly occupied with some insane practical joke or other were his happiest. Nevertheless it gave him some peace, and his wild eyes were not so terrible as those looks of anxiety that thirsted for salvation or the eternal torments of unrest. Often he would beat his head against the wall or bring about a violent physical pain through other means.

On the morning of the eighth of February he remained in bed. Oberlin went up to him and found him lying almost naked on the bed, violently agitated. Oberlin attempted to cover him, but Lenz complained terribly about how heavy everything was, how heavy! He did not think that he could walk. Now at last he experienced the monstrous weight of the air. Oberlin spoke to him of courage. Yet he remained in this condition for the greater part of the day, nor would he take any nourishment.

Toward evening Oberlin was called to a sick man in Bellefosse. The weather was mild and the moon was shining. On the way back he was met by Lenz. He seemed utterly rational and spoke with Oberlin in a quiet, friendly manner. He asked him not to walk too far; Lenz promised. Upon leaving he turned suddenly toward Oberlin and said rapidly:

"You see, Pastor Oberlin, if it weren't for that I would be much better off."

"If it weren't for what, my friend?"

"Don't you hear it? Don't you hear that dreadful cry that screams around all the horizon and which we generally call silence? Since I came to this silent valley I hear it all the time, it won't allow me to sleep; yes, Pastor Oberlin, if only I could sleep again!" He went off then, shaking his head.

Oberlin returned to Waldbach and wanted to send someone after him when he heard him climbing the stairs to his room. A moment later something plunged into the courtyard with such force that Oberlin could not possibly have thought it caused by the fall of a human body. The nurse rushed in deathly pale and trembling. . . .

He sat in the carriage with icy resignation as it drove through the valley in a westerly direction. It was all the same to him where he was driven. Several times when the carriage was endangered by the rough road he remained sitting in this state as they made their way through the mountains. Toward evening they arrived in Rheintal. They gradually left the mountains behind them, so that now they appeared like a deep blue wave of crystal rearing up into the sunset, and on whose warm flood the red rays of evening played. A shimmering blue mist lay across the plains at the foot of the mountains. It grew dark as they approached Strasbourg. The moon was high and full. All distant objects were dark; only the mountains formed a sharp contour on the horizon. The earth was a golden goblet out of which golden rays of moonlight overflowed. Lenz stared out quietly, without apprehensions or pressures, except for a hollow anxiety inside him that grew the more the objects outside became lost in darkness. At that time he made several attempts to do himself harm, but he was too closely watched.

The next morning, in dull, rainy weather, he arrived in Strasbourg. He seemed completely rational, spoke to people. He did everything that the others did; still there was a dreadful void inside him, he no longer felt any anxiety, nor any desire. His existence was an inevitable burden.

And so his life went on. . . .

THE HESSIAN COURIER

THE HESSIAN COURIER

FIRST REPORT

Darmstadt, in July 1834

INTRODUCTION

This paper is meant to inform the Hessian people, yet whoever speaks the truth will be hanged; yes, even the man who reads the truth may be punished by some perjured judge. For that reason those who receive this paper must be aware of the following:

1. They must carefully put this paper in a safe place outside their houses in order to preserve it from the police.

2. They may pass it on only to friends they can trust.

3. Those whom they cannot trust as surely as they can themselves may be given this paper anonymously and by secret means.

4. Should it be found on the person of anyone who has read it, then he must confess that he was just about to hand it over to the District Council.

5. Should this paper be found on the person of anyone who has not read it, then he, of course, is guiltless.

FREEDOM FOR THE HUTS!
WAR ON THE PALACES!

The life of the aristocrats is a long Sunday: they live in beautiful houses, they wear elegant clothes, they have fat faces, and they speak a language of their own; whereas the people lie at their feet like manure on the fields. The farmer follows his plow, while the aristocrat follows behind him and his plow and drives him on with the oxen pulling his plow; he takes the grain and leaves the farmer the stubble. The life of the farmer is a long workday. Strangers devour his fields before his very eyes, his body is a callus, his sweat the salt on the aristocrats' tables.

In the Grand Duchy of Hesse there are 718,373 inhabitants who yearly give to the state some 6,363,436 guilders in the form of:

1. Direct taxes	2,128,131 Guilders
2. Indirect taxes	2,478,264 Guilders
3. Fields	1,547,394 Guilders
4. Royal prerogatives	46,398 Guilders
5. Monetary fines	98,511 Guilders
6. Various sources	64,198 Guilders
	6,363,436 Guilders

This money is the blood-tithe being taken from the body of the people. Almost 700,000 human beings sweat, groan, and starve because of it. It is extorted in the name of the state, the extortionists refer themselves to the government, and the government replies that it is necessary for the maintenance of order in the state. What powerful organism is this thing: the state? Let a number of people live in a country where there are decrees or laws at hand according to which every man must regulate himself, and they say they are forming a state. The state, therefore, is *everyone*; the regulators of a state are its laws, through which the well-being of *everyone* is secured and which proceed from the well-being of *everyone*. Now see what the Grand Duchy has made of the state; see what they call it: maintaining order in the state! Seven hundred thousand human beings pay 6,000,000 guilders for it; that is, they are made into farmhorses and plow oxen so that they may live in order. To live in order means to starve and be exploited.

Who are they who have made this order and who are on guard to maintain it? They are the government of the Grand Duchy. The government is formed by the Grand Duke and his chief officials. The other officials are men who are appointed by the government to maintain this order. Its numbers are legion: councils of state, district magistrates, district councils, treasury officials, and forest officials, etc., each with its armies of secretaries, etc. The people are its herds, they are the people's shepherds, milkers, and fleecers. They wear the farmers' hides, the plunder of the poor is in their houses; widows' and orphans' tears are the grease on their faces; they rule freely and exhort the people to serfdom. These are the ones to whom you give the 6,000,000 in tribute; and for that they have the trouble of governing you; that is, they let themselves be fed by you and rob you of your human and civil rights. Do you now see the harvest of your sweat!

There are 1,110,607 guilders paid out to the Ministry of the Interior and the Justice Department. In return you have a chaos of laws arbitrarily accumulated from ordinances of all centuries, and generally written in foreign languages. The absurdity of all former generations has hereby descended upon you, the burden under which they expired continues in you. The law is the property of an insignificant class of aristocrats and learned men, a class which bestows its own authority on itself. This authority is merely a means to keep you in check, so that they can fleece you all the more easily; it speaks of laws you cannot understand, of principles that you know nothing of, judgments which you do not comprehend. It is incorruptible because it permits itself to be paid enough by you so that corruption is unnecessary. But the greater number of its servants are thoroughly bought off by the government. Their leisure is based on a pile of 461,373 guilders (the total expenses for courts of justice and prisons). The dress coats, sticks, and sabers of their unassailable servants are studded with 197,502 guilders of silver (a sum equal to the cost of maintaining the police, the constabulary, etc.) Justice in Germany has for centuries been the whore of German princes. Each step you take toward them must be paved with silver, and every decree paid for by you with poverty and humiliation. Consider the coupons for stamp duty, consider your bowing and scraping in magistrates' offices and your having to stand guard outside them. Consider the fees for court ushers and scribes. You may accuse your neighbor of stealing a potato, but try just once to complain about being subject to the caprice of a fat paunch and that this caprice is called law; complain that you are the farm horses of the state; complain about your lost rights as human beings: where are these courts of law that will take up your complaint, where the judges who administer their justice? The chains of your fellow citizens of Vogelsberg who were hauled off to Rockenburg will give you your answer.

For the Treasury you pay out 1,551,502 guilders. This pays for Treasury officials, the Chief Collector of Taxes, the Tax gatherer, and the Under Collector of Taxes. In return they keep records of the produce of your fields and count your heads. They tax the ground under your feet and the morsel in your mouth. In return these gentlemen sit around together in dress coats while the people stand before them naked and humiliated. They take stock of one's thighs and shoulders and determine how much more they can bear up under; and should they be compassionate, then it is only as one spares an animal which one feels should not be too much exhausted.

For the military you pay 914,820 guilders. In return your sons receive a colored jacket for their bodies, a weapon or a drum across their shoulders, and every fall have the privilege of shooting blindly once and telling how the gentlemen and the spoiled boys of the nobility excel the children of all other honorable people, and march around with them on broad city streets to the sounds of trumpets and drums. For these 900,000 guilders your sons must swear allegiance to the tyrants and stand guard at their palaces. With their drumming they drown out your sighs; with the butt ends of their rifles they break in your skulls should you dare to think that you are free human beings. They are lawful murderers protecting lawful robbers; consider what happened at Södel! In Vogelsberg your brothers and children were murderers of their own brothers and fathers.

Four hundred and eighty thousand guilders for government retirement pensions. In return officials are gently propped up with pillows if they have served the state faithfully for a certain time; that is, if they have eagerly served as underlings in this regular game of extortion which is called law and order.

One hundred and seventy-four thousand guilders for the Ministry of State and the State's Council. It is certain that today the greatest villains everywhere in Germany stand at the right hand of the princes, at least here in the Grand Duchy. Should an honorable man make his way

into the Council of State he would be properly expelled.
Yet could an honorable man be a minister now, or remain one, he would be nothing more, as matters stand in
Germany at present, than a puppet on strings manipulated
by the princely puppet, who in turn is manipulated by a
valet or a coachman, or by his wife and her minion,
or by his half-brother—or by all of them together.

Furthermore, for the Grand Duke's princely dwelling
and for his princely attire you must pay the sum of
827,772 guilders.

The institutions and the people of whom I have spoken
till now are nothing but instruments, servants. They do
nothing in their own names; under their appointments to
office is written an L., which signifies: Ludwig by the
grace of God; and when they speak they say with rever-
ence: "In the name of the Grand Duke." This is their
battle cry when they sell your effects at auction, drive off
your livestock, and throw you into prison. "In the name of
the Grand Duke," they say, and the person of whom they
speak is His Unassailable, Holy, Sovereign, Royal Highness. But approach this child of man and look through
his princely pretense. It eats when it is hungry, sleeps when
its eyes grow heavy. But know that it crept into this world
as naked and soft as you, and will be carried out as stiff
and cold as you, and yet it has its foot upon your necks,
has 700,000 people behind its plow, has ministers who are
answerable for everything it does, has power over your
property through the taxes which it prescribes, power over
your lives through the laws which it makes, it has about
it noble lords and ladies who are known as the court, and
his divine power is bequeathed to his children with wives
who are of equal godlike descent.

The prince is the head of the leech that creeps across
you, the ministers are its teeth, and the officials its tail.
The hungry bellies of all the aristocratic lords whom he
has put in high places are the bleeding-vessels which he
has set to catch the country's blood. That L. beneath their
appointments is the mark made by the beast which the
idolators of our time idolize. The royal robe is the carpet
on which the lords and ladies of the nobility and the
court roll upon one another in their lasciviousness—they

hide their running sores with ribbons and orders and cover their scabby bodies with precious clothes. The daughters of the people are their maids and whores, the sons of the people their lackeys and soldiers. Go to Darmstadt and see for yourself the good times these lords have on your money, and tell your starving wives and children that others are being well fed on their bread; tell them of the beautiful clothes dyed in their sweat, and of the decorative ribbons cut from the calluses on their hands; tell them of the stately houses erected from the bones of the people; and then creep back into your smoky huts and bend yourselves over stone-laden fields so that one day your children can go there too and see one heir to a reigning prince and his wife trying to give advice to another heir to another reigning prince; so that they can see through the open glass doors the tablecloth from which these lords eat, and smell the lamps which illuminate their rooms with the fat of the farmer.

For the Provincial Diet you pay 16,000 guilders.

In the year 1789 the people of France were tired of being the king's miserable jade. They raised themselves up and called together men whom they could trust, and these men joined together and said that a king is a man like all other men, he is merely the chief servant of the state, he must be responsible to the people, and if he administers his office badly he may be punished by the people. They then defined the Rights of Man: "No man may inherit by birth either privilege or title; no man by virtue of his property may obtain any privilege over any other man. The highest authority resides in the will of all men or of the majority. This will constitutes the law and it proclaims itself through the Provincial Diets or the representatives of the people, who are elected by all, and every man is eligible. These elected express the wills of their electors, and therefore the majority of wills among the elected is in accordance with the majority of wills among the people. The king has only to attend to the execution of the law proclaimed by them." The King swore to remain true to this Constitution; yet he perjured himself with the people, and the people condemned him as was befitting a traitor.

The French people then abolished hereditary kingship and
freely elected a new ruling body, under which every people
had its rights according to Reason and the Holy Scriptures.
The men whose function is to guard over the fulfillment
of the law were appointed by the convention of elected
representatives who formed a new ruling body. They con-
stituted the government and the lawgivers elected by the
people, and France was a Free State.

The remaining kings of Europe were horrified at the
violence demonstrated by the French people; they thought
they might all be ruined as the result of this one king
and that their maltreated subjects might be wakened by
the Frenchman's cry for freedom. They descended upon
France from all sides with powerful instruments of war
and vast resources, and the greater part of the nobility
and aristocracy revolted and joined with the enemy. The
people grew furious and rose up in all its strength. It
crushed the traitors and destroyed the mercenaries of the
kings. This new-won freedom grew in the blood of the
tyrants, and thrones trembled at their voices and the
people rejoiced. But the French themselves sold their new-
won freedom for the glory which Napoleon tendered them
and elevated him to the emperor's throne. Then the Almighty permitted the Emperor's army to freeze to death
in Russia and chastised France by means of the Cossacks'
terrorism and gave back to the French the fat-paunched
Bourbons for kings, so that France might convert herself
from its idolatry of hereditary kingship and serve God who
created Man free and equal. But when the time of its
punishment drew to a close and brave men in July 1830
ran the perjured King Charles X from the country, free
France, for all that, turned itself once again to a semi-
hereditary kingship and bound itself in the person of that
dissembler Louis Philippe to a new scourge. In Germany,
however, and in the remainder of Europe, there was great
rejoicing when Charles X was deposed, and the suppressed
German states armed themselves in the battle for freedom.
The princes deliberated together on how to escape the
fury of the people, and the crafty among them said: "Let
us hand over a part of our authority so that we may keep

the rest." And they appeared before the people and said: "We want to present you with the very freedom for which you are about to fight." And trembling with fear they threw down a few scraps and spoke of their mercy. Unfortunately the people trusted them and went to sleep. And so Germany was as deceived as France.

What, after all, are these constitutions in Germany? Gifts of straw from which the princes have threshed out the last piece of grain. What are our Provincial Diets? Slow-moving carts which once or twice we might be able to shove in the path of our princes' and our ministers' rapacity, but which can never build for us a solid foundation for German freedom. What are the laws of election? Encroachments upon the civil and human rights of almost all Germans. Consider the rules of election in the Grand Duchy, according to which no one may be elected unless he is extremely wealthy, no matter how upright or loyal he may be, and yet Grolmann was good enough for election, and it was he who wanted to steal 2,000,000 guilders from you.

You are paying 6,000,000 guilders to a handful of persons in the Grand Duchy to whose capricious attitude your lives and property are entrusted, and it is the same for all others in our dismembered Germany. You *are* nothing, you *have* nothing! You are divested of any rights. You must give what your insatiable oppressors demand, and bear up under that with which they burden you. Lift up your eyes and count the little band of your oppressors, whose only strength comes from the blood they suck from you, and from the arms which they borrow from you because you have no will of your own. There are perhaps 10,000 of them in the Grand Duchy, and there are 700,000 of you, and the same ratio holds true of all the rest of Germany. Indeed they may threaten you with implements and the mounted soldiers of kings, but I say to you: Whosoever raises a sword against the people, he shall also perish by the people's sword. Germany is now a field of battle, soon it will be a paradise. The German people is a *single* body, you are a member of it. It is immaterial where this seeming corpse begins to move and show signs of life. When the Lord gives you His sign through the men through whom He will lead the people from servitude into freedom, then raise yourselves up and the whole body will rise up with you.

DRAMABOOKS
(Plays)

Elmer Rice: Three Plays (Adding Machine, Street Scene, Dream Girl) (0735-5)
The Day the Whores Came Out to Play Tennis . . . by Arthur Kopit (0736-3)
Platonov by Anton Chekhov (0737-1)
Ugo Betti: Three Plays (The Inquiry, Goat Island, The Gambler) (0738-X)
Jean Anouilh Vol. 3 (Thieves' Carnival, Medea, Cécile, Traveler Without Lu
    Orchestra, Episode in the Life of an Author, Catch As Catch Can) (0739-8)
Max Frisch: Three Plays (Don Juan, The Great Rage of Philip Hotz, When the
    Was Over) (0740-1)
New American Plays Vol. 2 ed. by William M. Hoffman (0741-X)
Plays from Black Africa ed. by Fredric M. Litto (0742-8)
Anton Chekhov: Four Plays (The Seagull, Uncle Vanya, The Cherry Orchard,
    Three Sisters) (0743-6)
The Silver Foxes Are Dead and Other Plays by Jakov Lind (The Silver Foxes Are
    Anna Laub, Hunger, Fear) (0744-4)
New American Plays Vol. 3 ed. by William M. Hoffman (0745-2)
The Modern Spanish Stage: Four Plays, ed. by Marion Holt (The Concert at Saint
    Condemned Squad, The Blindfold, The Boat Without a Fisherman) (0746-0)
Life Is a Dream by Calderón (0747-9)
New American Plays Vol. 4 ed. by William M. Hoffman (0748-7)

THE NEW MERMAIDS

Bussy D'Ambois by George Chapman (1101-8)
The Broken Heart by John Ford (1102-6)
The Duchess of Malfi by John Webster (1103-4)
Doctor Faustus by Christopher Marlowe (1104-2)
The Alchemist by Ben Jonson (1105-0)
The Jew of Malta by Christopher Marlowe (1106-9)
The Revenger's Tragedy by Cyril Tourneur (1107-7)
A Game at Chess by Thomas Middleton (1108-5)
Every Man in His Humour by Ben Jonson (1109-3)
The White Devil by John Webster (1110-7)
Edward the Second by Christopher Marlowe (1111-5)
The Malcontent by John Marston (1112-3)
'Tis Pity She's a Whore by John Ford (1113-1)
Sejanus His Fall by Ben Jonson (1114-X)
Volpone by Ben Jonson (1115-8)
Women Beware Women by Thomas Middleton (1116-6)
Love for Love by William Congreve (1117-4)
The Spanish Tragedy by Thomas Kyd (1118-2)

SPOTLIGHT DRAMABOOKS

The Last Days of Lincoln by Mark Van Doren (1201-4)
Oh Dad, Poor Dad . . . by Arthur Kopit (1202-2)
The Chinese Wall by Max Frisch (1203-0)
Billy Budd by Louis O. Coxe and Robert Chapman (1204-9)
The Firebugs by Max Frisch (1206-5)
Andorra by Max Frisch (1207-3)
Balm in Gilead and Other Plays by Lanford Wilson (1208-1)
Matty and the Moron and Madonna by Herbert Lieberman (1209-X)
The Brig by Kenneth H. Brown (1210-3)
The Cavern by Jean Anouilh (1211-1)
Saved by Edward Bond (1212-X)
Eh? by Henry Livings (1213-8)
The Rimers of Eldritch and Other Plays by Lanford Wilson (1214-6)
In the Matter of J. Robert Oppenheimer by Heinar Kipphardt (1215-4)
Ergo by Jakov Lind (1216-2)
Biography: A Game by Max Frisch (1217-0)
Indians by Arthur Kopit (1218-9)
Narrow Road to the Deep North by Edward Bond (1219-7)
Ornifle by Jean Anouilh (1220-0)
Inquest by Donald Freed (1221-9)
Lemon Sky by Lanford Wilson (1222-7)
The Night Thoreau Spent in Jail by Jerome Laurence and Robert E. Lee (1223-5)

For a complete list of books of criticism and history of the drama, please writ
Hill and Wang, 72 Fifth Avenue, New York, New York 10011.